CHANDELIERS

CHANDELIERS

Elizabeth Hilliard

A Bulfinch Press Book

Little, Brown and Company

Boston   New York   London

To my father, David Hilliard

First United States Edition

ISBN 0-8212-2768-8
Library of Congress Control Number 2001090608

First published in Great Britain in 2001 by Mitchell Beazley, an imprint of Octopus Publishing Group Limited.

Bulfinch Press is an imprint and trademark of Little, Brown and Company (Inc.)

Printed and bound in China

*Previous page: With their waterfalls of drops, shimmering and twinkling in the light, these
scintillating creations embody the ultimate in chandelier design and technology.*
*Opposite: A hot-air balloon chandelier – an engaging eccentricity inspired by the ballooning exploits
of the Montgolfier brothers in the late eighteenth century – hanging from a gilded ceiling.*

CONTENTS

Left: *The brass chandelier in the dining room of Temple Newsam in Leeds, Yorkshire, was designed by G.F. Bodley and made by Watts & Co of London in 1877. Beneath its charming leaf and flower motifs hangs a weighty stabilizing ball with both pierced and engraved decoration.*

Right: *A magnificent chandelier hanging in the historic surroundings of the Castillo de Bendinas in Mallorca.*

The chandelier has a long and glorious history that has been largely ignored of late, probably due to it having been out of fashion for several decades until relatively recently. In the twenty-first century, however, the chandelier is once again assuming its rightful place as a positive choice of lighting fitting. Now we can look back over centuries of ingenuity and creativity to celebrate the breathtaking design and construction of these magnificent pieces, while at the same time looking forward to the chandelier's continued reinterpretation as a matchless element in interior decoration. No longer simply a provider (however handsome or beautiful) of light after sunset, the chandelier has become a sculptural presence, a visual stimulation, a statement of style, the first thing you notice as you enter a room.

This rediscovery and reinvention of the chandelier form was never a foregone conclusion. This book might easily have been a history of a decorative but outmoded curiosity. The history of chandeliers is indeed fascinating, rich in detail of advances in production methods and construction, illuminating about changing tastes and styles, revealing in anecdote. But the story is brought into sharp focus by arguments as to the contemporary relevance or otherwise of this type of fixture, now that its practical advantages have been superseded by the revolutionary technological and aesthetic advances in lighting science of the last few decades. Clearly we no longer need the chandelier, but do we still want it?

Today, decorating is about choice. Gone are the style police, bent on telling us that something or other will or won't do. Instead we can choose for

ourselves, opting for the extremes of severe minimalism or flamboyant opulence, or indeed anything in between. We can choose pure white or pale floaty tones, rich historic shades or bright primaries, or any mixture of these that happens to please us. And as for style, the choice is ours: kitsch or ethnic, colonial or baronial, classical or baroque – the list is endless.

Apart from matters of personal taste, probably the only constraint on our choice of interior decorating style today, and of the chandelier to go with it, is budget. In the past, however, social context, status and money went hand in hand, dictating the appearance and location – indeed the very existence – of each chandelier produced with such painstaking care.

The earliest chandeliers, of which very few survived the destruction of the Reformation in the sixteenth century, were to be found lending flickering light to the cavernous interiors of medieval churches and abbeys across Europe. The first chandeliers in private homes hung only in the palaces and mansions of the supremely wealthy and powerful. Apart from a guttering taper or the dim glow of firelight, illumination after sunset was largely beyond the means of most. So used are we now to the joys of electricity and tungsten halogen that we would find the interiors of any age before our own unremittingly gloomy.

The form taken by these early chandeliers was usually a wooden cross or a more sophisticated ring or crown of bronze or brass, with metal prickets – sharp points – on to which wax candles were pushed. These Romanesque or Gothic styles were to experience a resurgence of popularity in the nineteenth century. Then came the curly-armed brass forms, with which we are familiar from the exquisite Dutch and Flemish paintings of the fifteenth, sixteenth, and seventeenth centuries. From van Eyck through Dou to Vermeer, chandeliers are shown hanging in the homes of the prosperous merchant classes. More modest households, with access to the raw materials for candlemaking, might have had chandeliers made from turned wood, bent metal, wrought iron, or tin sheet – the latter being a distinctive feature of pioneering lighting fixtures in America.

Pretty and curvaceous glass chandeliers began to be made on the Venetian island of Murano around 1700. At the same time, the cut-glass or lead-crystal chandelier emerged in England and across Europe, a consequence

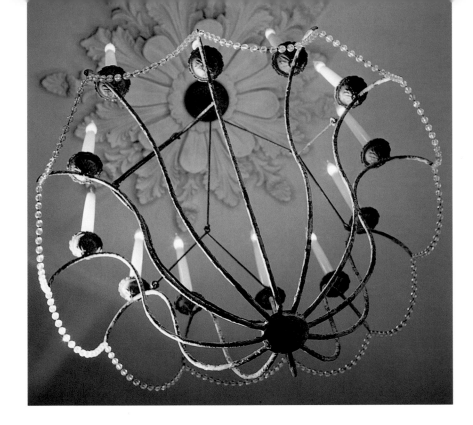

of advances in glassmaking technology, notably in the glass houses of London. At first these types of glass chandelier aimed to emulate the scintillating glamour of early rock-crystal chandeliers that were to be found only in the homes of the fabulously rich. The great age of the chandelier was reached in the eighteenth and nineteenth centuries, when lead crystal concoctions sparkled and shimmered in ballrooms and drawing rooms across Europe and America, shedding warm candlelight accompanied, in our imaginations, by the sound of music, murmuring voices, and the rustle of silk gowns.

These chandeliers were more than mere lighting appliances: they were works of art. For the first time, the names of individual manufacturers (who were also initially their own designers) began to appear – William Parker, William Perry, and F. & C. Osler in England (all these are also well reputed in India, Persia, and America), Baccarat in France, the Mount Washington Glass Factory in America, and many more. The chandelier offered social cachet; and those made by the best companies brought even greater kudos. The growing middle-class market, meanwhile, was satisfied by more accessible versions, in both scale and cost. Styles changed, from the light-as-air romanticism of Parker's neoclassical creations, with their tapering arms and delicate beaded necklaces, to the solid magnificence of the Regency tent-and-bag or tent-and-waterfall forms. What did not change was the social significance of these objects. The chandelier was always an expression of status.

Traditional forms of glass chandelier remained popular into the early twentieth century, partly because the alternatives in interior decoration – whether Arts and Crafts, Art Nouveau, Art Deco, or Modernism – generally opted for other forms of lighting. Although Modernism produced a few lighting fittings that can justifiably be called chandeliers in that they use multiple bulbs,

fragmenting light for effect, on the whole these movements preferred pendant lights with fabric, metal, wood, or glass shades. Two world wars and the subsequent drive for fresh forms for every element of the domestic interior brought the chandelier back to life, in the work of Italians Gino Sarfatti and Achille Castiglioni. Designers such as these revelled in the new materials and methods of industrial manufacture that emerged as an unexpected bonus of investment in the war effort. Their modern versions of the chandelier proved to have staying power: the Italian lighting company Flos still includes designs by Sarfatti and Castiglioni in the range it offers to the public.

The 1970s and 1980s might so easily have brought about the end of the chandelier. The two prevailing strands of fashionable interior decoration at this time were the self-consciously modern and the comfortingly traditional, the latter complete with floral printed cottons and ruched Austrian blinds. In either case, table lamps and wall- or ceiling-mounted surface spotlights were de rigueur. If you were very advanced, you might install recessed spotlights, perhaps with a bulbous protrusion like an eyeball. The 1990s were refreshingly honest by comparison, with the emphasis in interior decoration shifting to uncluttered authenticity, either contemporary in style (pared-down surfaces, real wood, glass, or concrete, converted industrial buildings) or historic in inspiration

(limewash and distemper, shutters and blinds, distressed furniture). In this free-breathing atmosphere, the era of choice had begun.

Never in the long history of the chandelier has there been as much choice as there is today. At the top end of the market, not only can you have a Sarfatti design in your home, or commission an uncompromisingly contemporary chandelier from one of the new wave of lighting designers, but you can also choose the latest contemporary crystal creation from the same Baccarat glass house that was founded in 1765. You can have an exact replica of the historic Thornton crystal chandelier, made in England in 1732 and currently in the Winterthur Museum, Delaware, made for you by specialists Wilkinson plc of London. You can choose from any number of exquisite original glass creations from the famously enchanting emporia of Denton (alias Mrs Crick) in London or Nesle in New York. You can buy, over the internet or in person, a chandelier made under licence from colonial Williamsburg, Virginia, by Period Lighting or, in the spirit of historic chandeliers, from Framburg, Hobe Sound, or Schonbek in the USA, or Barovier & Toso on Murano. Massive wrought-iron

Left: *Coloured glass offers yet further scope for decorative flourishes: here a gilded metal chandelier is festooned with glass beads of different colours and pressed coloured glass fruit, including bunches of grapes.*

Right: *The colours of this glass chandelier hanging in a kitchen are echoed by the tiles and cupboard doorknobs – demonstrating that with sensitive treatment chandeliers can provide an effective lighting solution in even the most unexpected spaces.*

chandeliers, 3m (10ft) tall by over 1.5m (5ft) wide, are once again in production (made by Stuart Interiors, England) and so are frolics such as the chandeliers imitating hot-air balloons (McCloud Lighting, England) that were originally created to celebrate the first flights by the Montgolfier brothers in 1783.

Alternatively, to suit a more modest budget, you can scour the brocante stalls in French markets or the junk shops of England for a pretty glass or handsome Gothic-style brass chandelier, possibly as old as Victorian. You could also buy an inexpensive Dutch- or French-style fitting from a high-street store. Simple painted iron and untreated metal chandeliers are available from countless modern furniture and department stores. There seems no end to choice, which increases as new genres are rediscovered, such as the sparkling coloured glass chandeliers once so beloved of Indian rajahs and Persian princes.

The aim of this book is to inform and inspire. To offer an insight into the history and changing style of the chandelier through almost five centuries. To provide the ultimate style guide as well as practical details. To bring to life these wonderful objects, and to help you choose a style of chandelier for your home. Whatever your choice, when you hang a chandelier you acquire something beautiful and practical and also an object that will became a focus for the room. Other decorations will revolve around it. It will become a centrepiece,

Left: *A bizarre and wonderful chandelier, one of a pair made of wrought and painted iron with glass shades, finds a fitting backdrop in the carved marble fire surround in the Drawing Room of Cragside, Northumbria. Complete with its chandeliers, the room was ceremonially opened in 1884 in the presence of the Prince and Princess of Wales, later Edward VII and Queen Alexandra. The house and grounds are now owned by the National Trust and open to the public.*

Above: *A witty contemporary variation on the chandelier theme, 85 Lamps by Rodi Graumans of Droog Design, hangs over the dining table in Jan Des Bouvrie's house in St Tropez, France.*

Right: *A pretty contemporary steel chandelier, delicately decorated with glass beads.*

Far right: *This large and spectacular gilded brass and crystal chandelier, measuring some 3m (9¾ ft) high and weighing 600kg (272 lb), was made in 1995 by the Czech company Preciosa Lustry – one of the worlds largest manufacturers of lighting and chandeliers – for the main lobby of the Merchant Court Hotel in Bangkok. The hotel was destroyed by fire in the same year, reopening only in 1999. Following painstaking refurbishment work by the Preciosa Lustry team, the fire-damaged chandelier has been restored to its original splendour.*

a talking point, just as a fireplace draws attention at a lower level in a room, so a chandelier is the highest point of a room's decoration.

Today, we have at our disposal the full gamut of technical advances in lighting; these allow us to control the colour of light and its strength, so ensuring that a room has all the light and shade it needs. This is not entirely a new idea. Light from the central chandelier was routinely supplemented in earlier ages by wall sconces and candlesticks as a matter of necessity. Now, however, the quality and abundance of light in our homes means that we can lend free reign to our imaginations, venturing way beyond practical considerations, important though these are. The chandelier hanging from your ceiling – whether primarily of crude wrought iron or nylon fibre optics woven into frayed nylon, of hand-blown glass or "found" objects, of elegant lead crystal or playful coloured glass – can define and fulfil your lighting (and decorating) fantasies as part of a wider lighting (and decorating) scheme.

We have entered the new age of the chandelier: long may it last.

EARLY LIGHTING

The earliest chandeliers (though the name did not come

until much later) were the "crowns" of light used to illuminate

the Romanesque churches and cathedrals of medieval Europe.

Suspended wooden lighting fixtures were also to be found

in the palaces and castles of the very wealthy and powerful.

Centuries later, across the Atlantic in the New World, simple

and attractive chandeliers in wood and metal reflected

the resourcefulness of the early pioneers.

Previous page left:
The remarkable chandelier in Bristol Cathedral, dating from c.1460 and made from laten (a metal alloy similar to brass).

Previous page right:
A detail of the Bristol Cathedral chandelier showing St George triumphant over the dragon.

Above: *A pair of monumental double crown chandeliers, medieval in inspiration and made in England by Stuart Interiors, on a scale appropriate to the size of this baronial hall, newly created in Connecticut. The owner was inspired by a visit to Stratford-upon-Avon in England, where he fell under the spell of the architecture and style of the late Middle Ages.*

Right: *Chandeliers are rarely seen from above: this view reveals in close-up the unusual design of this delicate iron fixture.*

U ntil relatively recently, the world was indeed a place of darkness. Most people relied on one regular source of light: the sun. Once it had set, the flames of a fire (if they had one) and perhaps a tallow taper might offer some light. Most did not enjoy even this luxury, and at night total darkness reigned. From the Roman empire to the Middle Ages and after, the great majority of people in Europe lived by the sun, rising with the dawn and eating their main meal at dusk, retiring immediately afterward for the night.

The first chandeliers were to be found in places of worship, and later in the dwellings of an exalted few. In the late eighth century, Pope Hadrian is reputed to have presented St Peter's Basilica in the Vatican City with a chandelier capable of holding an astonishing 1,400 candles. An early medieval example in the Palatine Chapel at Aix-la-Chapelle has prickets (upright metal spikes for securing candles) and cups for oil and wick arranged alternately on an iron hoop. In the eleventh and twelfth centuries, chandeliers documented in Germany, the Netherlands, and France also took the form of great suspended metal wheels, like crowns. A thirteenth-century inventory of St Paul's Cathedral in London describes a hammered iron corona, with floral decoration. Iron chandeliers were also decorated with polychrome paint, jewels and enamelwork.

Simpler timber forms remained in use, none the less, even in the most illustrious households. As late as the fifteenth century, the court of Charles VI of France was lit by a primitive-looking cross-beam chandelier. A contemporary manuscript, now in the British Museum, shows ladies in court costume watching a masque performed by fur-clad entertainers beneath a simple "X" shape timber construction, directly descended from the medieval candlebeam. A large round weight hangs under the wood to steady it, and a ring beneath was presumably used to pull it down when new candles were needed. At the top of each end of the cross-bar is a small dish, forerunner to the drip pan, holding a candle secured in place by a pricket. Similar arrangements with two candles on each arm were known as "double candlesticks". As late as the end of the 1540s, a wooden candlebeam of this type was considered worthy of mention in a post mortem inventory of the estate of the English king Henry VIII.

Chandeliers of silver and gold are also recorded in contemporary inventories of the possessions of wealthy and powerful individuals, and of the

church. In the later medieval period, Durham Cathedral boasted an example with "three marveilous faire silver Basins hung in chains of silver" (Rites of Durham, n.d.), each with a lining of less precious metal for catching the dripping candle wax. The candles were constantly renewed and never extinguished, "in token that the House was always watchinge to God".

In contemporary descriptions of chandeliers the word "latten" or "laten" often appears. This was a metal alloy approximating to brass (an alloy of copper and zinc, known to this day in French as *laiton*), though metal processing at this time was an inexact science that was to improve only gradually over the centuries. Until 1466 (when it was sacked by Philip the Good, Duke of Burgundy), the main centre of production for brass-type metals was Dinant, in the Meuse region of what is now Belgium. From here, metal goods (known as dinanderie) and sheet metal were exported across Europe.

Importing countries included England, which at this time had no significant indigenous brass production. The few surviving medieval chandeliers in Britain, all similar in form, are almost certainly examples of dinanderie. Two are of particular interest. The first now hangs in Bristol Cathedral, having survived the wartime bombing of its previous home at the nearby Temple Church. The second is to be found in the chapel of the Royal Foundation of St Katharine, a religious foundation dating from 1147 and currently based in Limehouse, east London. The Bristol chandelier is typical for its date (around 1460), with two figures: the Virgin, crowned and cradling the infant Jesus, and, below her on the base, St George spearing the dragon. The plinth on which the Virgin stands is supported by a series of uprights, so that St George is effectively imprisoned in a loose cage. Candle arms, each a short "S" shape with delicately curving leaves forming a quatrefoil, branch out in two tiers from the bases of the statues and the bottom is fitted with a ring, a standard feature enabling the chandelier to be pulled down for maintenance. Advances in candle manufacture at this time meant that candles could be produced to a standard size, which has led, in this case, to the inclusion of candle nozzles rather than prickets. Charming and refined, it offers a seductive contrast to the utilitarian candlebeams and massive rings and crowns that had come before.

Above: *A charming modern interpretation of the medieval crown chandelier, 78cm (2½ ft) in diameter, designed and made by McCloud Lighting in England.*

Left: *This elegant forged iron crown chandelier in a pared-down modern variation of the Gothic style is displayed to great effect in a converted barn in the Cotswolds.*

While recognizably similar to the Bristol chandelier, the example at St Katharine's is at the same time startlingly different. It has the same cage structure, with the top supporting a statue and the bottom finished with a ring. Gone, however, are the prettily curving arms and leaves, in favour of a single tier of short arms embellished only with a kink at their halfway points. Gone, too, are the religious figures. Most extraordinarily of all, the supporting uprights are decorated with classical busts. Believed to have been the gift of John Holland, Duke of Exeter, who died in 1457 after a colourful military life, it is roughly contemporary with the Bristol example.

The marked difference between the two has fascinated and preoccupied numerous researchers in recent decades, including most notably the Tudor historian Victor Chinnery and the lighting designer and consultant Kevin McCloud. They have concluded that the St Katharine's chandelier once had the same accoutrements as the Bristol chandelier, but was adapted in the early seventeenth century to accommodate post-Reformation sentiments. The statue of the Virgin was a clear example of popery that had to go. The quatrefoil leaves, being Gothic in inspiration, were also unacceptable and were laboriously replaced with plain arms. The busts are representations of the Caesars, a safely classical reference. In other words, as Kevin McCloud has observed, "the piece has been de-consecrated and modernised to suit the post-Reformation age of Renaissance Classicism".

Centuries later, there was a strong revival of interest in the very Gothicism that was removed from the St Katharine's chandelier. From the mid-eighteenth century, the movement now known as the Gothic Revival swept the western world. It had its origins in Britain (indeed, in *The Gothic Revival*, published in 1928, Kenneth Clark described it as "perhaps the only purely English movement in the plastic arts") but influenced architecture and the decorative arts across Europe and America. A pair of brass and crystal lighting fixtures of 1840-50, now in the Historic New Orleans Collection, are among the finest surviving examples of American Gothic Revival chandeliers. Beneath their fringing prisms there is a rising sequence of detailed crowns, the bottom two supporting tiers of candles whose drip pans carry similarly fine decoration.

Above: *One of the Gothic Revival chandeliers (originally powered by gas) designed by the Scottish architect John Hyppolyte Blanc for his decorative scheme for the Great Hall of Edinburgh Castle (1887-90). The cage form of the central part and the quatrefoil leaves curving off the arms indicate that he had studied authentic Gothic chandeliers.*

Left: *A dramatic view of a sumptuous double crown chandelier in the type of setting to which such fittings are so well suited: large and spacious, with a lofty ceiling.*

Next page left: *This rare and intriguing fifteenth-century laten chandelier hangs in the chapel of the Royal Foundation of St Katharine, founded in 1147. Originally it was similar in appearance to the Bristol Cathedral chandelier (right), but was altered during the Reformation to remove popish and Gothic references.*

Next page right: *This pre-Reformation laten chandelier dates from around 1460 and hangs in Bristol Cathedral. It is surmounted by a figure of the Virgin, crowned and dandling the infant Jesus, with St George spearing the dragon beneath them.*

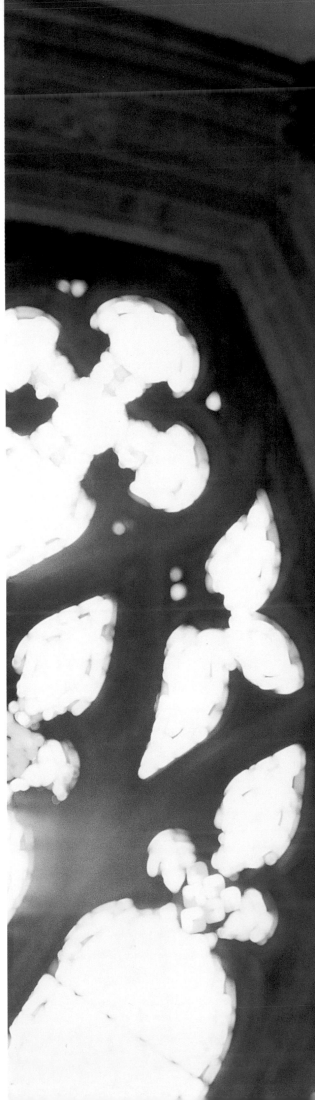

In Scotland, as in England, there was great enthusiasm for the Gothic Revival. One of the foremost Scottish architect-decorators of the late nineteenth century was John Hyppolyte Blanc. Born in Scotland to a shoemaker from Avignon and an Irish mother, Blanc became a national medallist at the Edinburgh School of Design. His subsequent career as an architect has lapsed into almost total oblivion as a result of the destruction of virtually all his records, drawings, and other papers in a series of disasters, culminating in the World War II bombing of the bonded warehouse in Manchester in which his archives were stored. Nor have his interiors fared much better, with the notable exception of his scheme for the Great Hall of Edinburgh Castle (1887-90), the recent restoration of which has revealed his unmistakable familiarity with original Gothic lighting fixtures, such as the chandelier in Bristol Cathedral.

By 1883, the Great Hall had suffered decades of use as an army hospital, which had involved the insertion of two extra floors. In this year, extensive evidence was found of the original medieval hall as it had been around the time when James IV of Scotland married Margaret Tudor of England in 1503. John Hyppolyte Blanc also found inspiration in *The Thissill and the Rois*, a poetic celebration of the marriage written in the same year by William Dunbar, who used the thistle to symbolize the Scots King and the rose

Above: *This unusual
turned wood and metal
wire chandelier, each arm
decorated with a single
wooden bead, has the
home-made charm of
so many pioneering
lighting fitments.*

his Tudor queen. Blanc incorporated this visual reference into his scheme for the Great Hall, notably in his designs for the lighting fixtures. These chandeliers (originally gasoliers and now electrified) display a "cage" form and quatrefoil leaf decorations traceable to the earlier dinanderie chandeliers.

Recent conservation work on these chandeliers has revealed that their cast-brass cores were painted verdigris green, with enamelled shields on each lamp in jewel-like colours. Copper branches each sported a cast-brass thistle head on which the gas flame was lit. Just as the stonework of England's medieval cathedrals was once brilliantly painted in polychrome (of which remnants may still be seen in places such as the rood screen in Lincoln Cathedral), so these chandeliers were designed to recapture the ebullience of a regal medieval interior. Blanc's chandeliers, in turn, are only now emerging from many decades of mistreatment. Until recently the British Army used the room as an armory, painting everything, including the chandeliers, a uniform black – perhaps a fitting symbol of the obscurity into which the work of their maker has fallen.

A hundred or so years after the building of the Great Hall, in the early seventeenth century, European adventurers began to settle in the New World. Virginia was colonized and Jamestown founded in 1607. In 1620 the Pilgrim Fathers landed in New England. The settlers brought with them a rich variety of architectural traditions and decorative styles. Naturally, they reproduced these familiar forms in their new objects and artifacts, using whatever materials came to hand, unhindered by the weight of conformity that burdened craftsmen in their native lands. While making visual references to European forms, early American chandeliers display a charming honesty and playfulness of form. Often they incorporate not only iron and turned wood but also wirework and shapes and straps snipped out of tin sheeting, sometimes crimped or ridged in places for greater reflectivity and decorative effect. On occasion the woodwork, and indeed the metal, is also finished with painted colour, either plain or patterned.

The chandeliers created by several of the first generations of American settlers are a visual delight. Many of them, however, were lost in the early twentieth century, when antique iron lighting devices were relegated to scrap metal by the ready availability of electricity. Most of those that survived joined the piles of raw materials collected for use in the wartime production of armaments for the defence and liberation of Europe. Thus, any genuine item of antique iron lighting equipment is a treasure indeed. Salvaged early American chandeliers are now preserved in fine collections of folk art and artifacts such as the Henry Francis du Pont Winterthur Museum, Delaware, Old Sturbridge Village, Massachusetts, and the Henry Ford Museum, Dearborn, Michigan.

An early type of American wrought-iron, hanging candle-holder consists of a tall central stem with a hook at the top for hanging it. The base of the stem divides into four upturned branches, each ending in a nozzle for holding a candle. For the time, however, this would have been a sophisticated piece as candles were mostly unheard of among poorer people, who instead used dried sticks of resinous pitch pine, known as candlewood or touchwood, which shed a good light but smoked terribly and dripped a sort of tar. Jammed into a crevice between stones in the fire surround, a stick of this sort would provide just enough light for the family to continue their activities into the evening.

Wrought iron was quickly superseded by tinned sheet iron as the favoured material for making chandeliers. Initially, in the eighteenth and early nineteenth centuries this was made in Pontypool in Wales and exported from Bristol into eastern seaboard cities such as New York, Philadelphia, Boston, and

Above: *This simple four-branch wrought-iron chandelier (with an interesting ratchet mechanism for raising and lowering it) looks ancient but is actually modern, made by craftsman Chris Payne for artist Kitty North, in whose dining room it hangs.*

Newport. Tin sheet was easy to work by cutting, punching, and bending; it was also hard-wearing and relatively inexpensive. The job of creating tin lighting appliances fell to dedicated tinsmiths who often peddled their wares, and therefore had the incentive to produce chandeliers that would seduce customers with their airy, elegant forms. They would also, no doubt, work to commission.

Probably the most common form of tin chandelier, especially on the East Coast, was the "double cone", with a central support consisting of two cones of bent tin sheet placed broad ends together to make a sort of diamond form. The two cones were not always identical in height, as is shown by the eight-armed example in the back parlour of the Clark-Haskell House in Lisbon, Connecticut, with its top cone flatter than the bottom one. From the lower cone there curved, like outstretched arms, tin straps, typically folded over at the edge for greater strength and rigidity. At the end of each arm was a candle nozzle and drip pan, some pinched or fluted like little pastry cups. Double-cone styles of chandelier are still made today by American "heritage" lighting companies.

An extraordinary example of the double cone may be seen in the Winterthur Museum in Delaware, its body decorated with bands and circles executed in tiny perforations in the tin. The eight tall "S"-shaped arms are of wire rather than strips of metal, and the effect is something like a cross between an Orthodox church censer and a joyfully flailing octopus. Probably made as recently as the late nineteenth century, this chandelier with its punched decorations seems to represent an exhilarating celebration of the nature of the material, which at that time was machine-made in large quantities.

Above left: *An airy chandelier with a turned wooden baluster at the centre and long, elegantly curving metal arms. This contemporary copy of an eighteenth-century Swedish design hangs in a house in Edinburgh, Scotland.*

Left: *A lively early American chandelier made from wire and tin sheet, probably as late as the early nineteenth century, and now in the Henry Francis du Pont Winterthur Museum in Delaware. Its striking double cone is punched with naive rythmic patterns and its arms wave cheerfully.*

Above: *A simple tin ring with four candle-holders above and antique crystal drops below, all suspended on chains, designed and made by Nigel Hoskins. The owner had it for sale in her shop but couldn't bear to part with it, so it now hangs in her bedroom in Lancashire, England.*

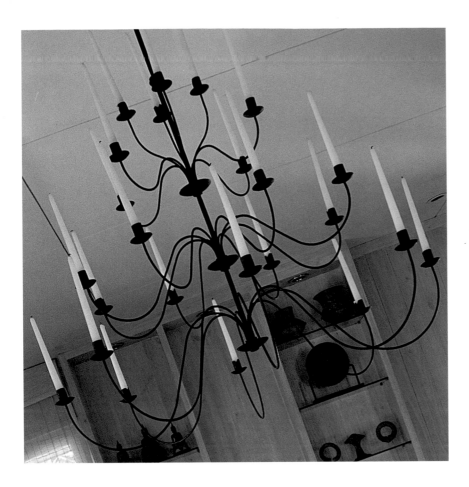

Less typical but even more festive are tin chandeliers in the form of a crown, with a band created from a strip of sheet metal curved into a loop. This is decorated with perforations, crimped edges, strips of metal, or erect leaf shapes, and from it sprout the candle-bearing arms. The effect is joyful, rustic, and irreverent. A fine example of this type of chandelier may be seen in the Museum for the Arts of Decoration at Cooper Union College in New York City. An early American version of the iron ring or crown has a hoop of strap metal twisted evenly around the entire circumference (a tribute to the steady hand and skill of the blacksmith who made it), adding a transforming touch of decorative humour to an otherwise solid and handsome piece. An eighteenth-century example of this type may be seen in the Winterthur Museum, Delaware.

Metal wire proved equally tractable, and wood was available locally in abundance. Well into the nineteenth century, a simple but elegant chandelier might be made from a turned wooden baluster – not unlike a newel post reduced in scale – to which were attached arms of metal wire curled into arabesques, with either forged metal candle spikes or turned wooden nozzles and drip pans. A striking example of this type of chandelier hangs in Coppock Great Hall, which is in a privately owned house in the Delaware River Valley: here the central wooden baluster is almost straight, like a simple table leg, with a few turned but modest protrusions and a plain round knop at the bottom.

Far left: *This elegant wire chandelier, modern but historical in inspiration, recalls neoclassical crystal chandeliers in its outlines and early American or Swedish examples in its materials. Designed by Gerald Pearce of Jim Thompson, it hangs in his own home in Bangkok.*

Left: *A charming antique iron chandelier with arms sprouting in triplets from a spherical base. It hangs in a kitchen at Kentwell, England.*

The protrusions are pierced by the ends of elegantly curving wire arms arranged in three tiers, eight on the bottom, six in the middle, and three on the top. As it is quite tall it hangs low in the room, where its light would be most useful for practical purposes. The candle nozzles are simple cylinders and the drip pans small and plain. The overall effect is airy and unpretentious yet quite beguiling.

More elaborate examples of this type of historic wood-and-wire American chandelier are decorated in a variety of delightful ways. Sometimes the arms are threaded with wooden balls or pear-shaped drops, the baluster is carved with leaves and other patterns, or it sports feathery leaves cut from sheet metal attached at intervals. The drip pan at the end of a wire arm may be supported by several twisted wires, and the baluster may be elaborately turned or brightly painted. Seized with enthusiasm, the makers of these chandeliers used them as an opportunity to celebrate the wonder of light and the sheer joy of survival in the face of the dangers of pioneering life. As well as outstanding examples of applied folk art, they are also powerfully symbolic objects.

Williamsburg, meanwhile, has an unequalled collection of historic chandeliers of quite a different sort. This town in Virginia, now restored as a national monument, was the capital of the British colonial government in the eighteenth century. It was also here that the Virginia legislators endorsed the Resolution for American Independence. Until independence, the governor was the king's representative in the colonies and his residence, the Governor's Palace, symbolized the dignity and importance of the British crown. Of all its numerous chandeliers, the most outstanding is a splendid and highly unusual silver creation that lights not a massive reception room but the small dining room. There is no other chandelier like this in the United States, and few in the rest of the world. The work of the English master silversmith Daniel Garnier between 1691 and 1697, it was owned by the British crown and in 1721 hung in St James's Palace (one of five silver chandeliers known to have hung in British royal palaces at that time). Later it lit Keele Hall in Staffordshire, and finally found its way to Williamsburg: evidence that such monumental pieces were considered as movable items like any other piece of furniture. The solid, masculine style of this chandelier is known as "Huguenot", after the French

Above: An exotic and unusual design in metal and gilded wood, just one example of the great variety of graceful forms to which chandeliers lend themselves.

Left: A bizarre and wonderful electric chandelier (known as an electrolier), designed by Robert Lorimer. It hangs in the house of Ardkinglas in Scotland, one of the first country houses in Britain to have electric power installed, with flamboyant fittings that could not fail to draw attention to the wonders of modern technology. This eclectic extravaganza includes figures of St George and the dragon amid a plethora of shells, hearts, basketwork and other decorative motifs.

Above: *An unusual antique six-arm silver chandelier, fitted with candles and shades, in an exotically decorated private apartment.*

Right: *This fabulous silver chandelier, made in about 1690 by the royal goldsmith George Garthorne, is one of an outstanding collection of chandeliers on view to the public at Hampton Court Palace in England. A silver chandelier of similar Huguenot design hangs in the Governor's Palace at Williamsburg, Virginia.*

Huguenot Protestants, many of them skilled craftsmen and women, who fled to England in order to escape persecution after Louis XIV's revocation of the Edict of Nantes (which had ensured their freedom of worship in Roman Catholic France) in 1685.

A similar though more massive silver chandelier may be seen at Hampton Court Palace in England, another palace with an outstanding collection of chandeliers. Bigger, longer, and with two tiers of arms to Williamsburg's one, it was made in about 1690 by the royal goldsmith George Garthorne. Across the world, only a handful of silver chandeliers have survived the centuries. These include two in the Moscow Kremlin (c.1734, by Paul de Lamerie), one made for Schloss Charlottenburg in Berlin (c.1730, by Johann Christian Lieberkühn), with figures of horses between the arms, and at least one by the Englishman John Bodington, with arms which bifurcate near the candle nozzles.

Among the famous silver chandeliers of which only reports survive are those created for the French royal family by Pierre Germain, who died in Paris in 1684. These included six for the chapel at Fontainebleau and an extraordinary example for the dauphin's quarters at Versailles, consisting of movable arms attached to eight human heads (made of silver).

In the late seventeenth century, gilded wooden chandeliers became popular in England and the rest of Europe as a less costly but comparably impressive alternative to their rock-crystal or silver-gilt counterparts. Wood allowed intricately carved patterns, but the arms had to be solid, especially where they joined the stem, in order to withstand the necessary leverage. Popular details included fluting, acanthus leaves, pendant tassels, gadrooned vases, and double-"C"-scrolled arms. Later, exotic features such as Indian masks and pineapples appeared. Sometimes an eagle stood proud on the topmost point. In both their massive swaggering presence and their carved detail, these gilded wooden chandeliers resemble not only the silver chandeliers of the period but also the decorative elements characteristic of its furniture. Some of the most impressive examples of this type of chandelier surviving in England are at Tabley House, Cheshire (c.1730), in the Stone Hall at Houghton, Norfolk (c.1740), and a remarkable piece at Speke Hall, Merseyside (c.1710), festooned with strings of wooden beads in imitation of the necklaces on a rock-crystal chandelier.

BRASS CHANDELIERS

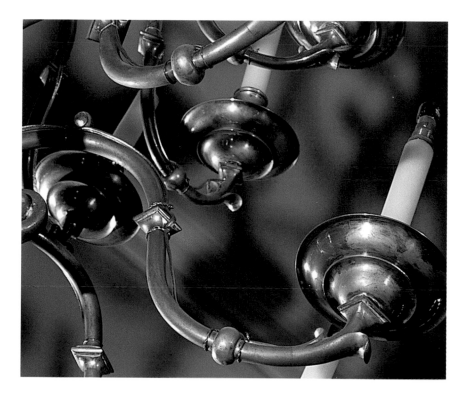

Of all metals and materials, gold is the most precious and

desirable. But this very rarity and costliness puts it far out

of reach for most domestic ornamentation, except perhaps

for a little gold leaf on decorative gesso. Brass offers the

same opulent warmth, however, with the added advantages

of being economically viable and wonderfully workable. This

has made brass chandeliers among the most practical and

popular throughout history.

Brass has been used to make light fittings for centuries, owing its popularity largely to the fact that it has the same warm and precious appearance as gold, but without its price. It is also eminently workable, lending itself to forging, casting, hammering, rolling, and extruding, so assuming a great variety of forms that may then be further decorated by means of chasing and engraving. It also retains a highly polished finish that reflects and thus amplifies any light source placed near to it.

An alloy of copper and zinc, brass was used by the Romans for their coins before AD100, but it is believed to have originated over a century earlier somewhere in the Middle East or around the Mediterranean, as a by-product of alchemical experiments devoted to the glamorous but sinister quest for the secret of transmuting base metals into gold.

Brass chandeliers have been used to light churches and other places of worship since the medieval period. In the early fifteenth century, Antwerp Cathedral alone is reputed to have contained no fewer than 400 brass chandeliers. However, of these medieval brass chandeliers survived the Reformation that swept Europe in the sixteenth century. In England, the crucial years were the 1530s. In 1533 the marriage of Henry VIII and Catherine of Aragon was declared null, and the following year Henry asserted his supremacy over the English church. The year 1536 saw the dissolution of the smaller monasteries, followed three years later by the redistribution of the huge wealth and extensive lands of the larger religious foundations. Within a decade, chandeliers that had hung untouched for centuries in holy places found themselves in houses and castles across the country, if they were lucky. A few were adapted to obliterate popish references, for example the St Katharine's chandelier in the previous chapter, and many others were destroyed.

Yet as early as 1434, when Jan van Eyck completed his famous portrait of Giovanni Arnolfini and his wife, now in the National Gallery in London, brass chandeliers were to be found in wealthy private homes. Arnolfini displays his with almost as much pride as he shows off his new wife. The Dutch masters

Previous page left: A brass chandelier in the Dutch style, with arms curving off a central stem and balanced by a large brass ball.

Previous page right: Detail of the Dutch style brass chandelier shown left.

Left: Another example of an Antique design with a central reservoir, this chandelier hangs in a former school building in Manhattan, refurbished internally for a private client by John Stefanidis.

Above: This four-light bronze chandelier in the style of an Antique lamp lights the stairwell of The Argory in County Armagh, Northern Ireland. Originally designed to be powered by colza oil (hence the vase-shaped central reservoir), it was thriftily converted to home-produced acetylene gas in about 1915. The candles are in fact sham sleeves designed to cover the gas burners. In an unusual arrangement, the chandelier's pair hangs directly above it. The house is owned by the National Trust and open to the public.

who followed van Eyck in the seventeenth century also often depict brass chandeliers in domestic settings. *The Young Mother*, for example, painted in about 1658 by the Dutch artist Gerrit Dou, shows a brass chandelier hanging in the room where the young woman is attempting to suckle her baby. It takes a form which is thought of to this day as Dutch in style, with six arms attached to the central stem or baluster above a large brass ball. The arms curl down around the ball so that the candlelight is reflected most effectively around the room. The other furnishings in the room and the clothes the woman wears indicate that this is a wealthy home.

The origins of the Dutch brass chandelier form have been the cause of much speculation. It bears no relation to the crowns, rings, and crosses of the medieval period, nor to the lantern shape of dinanderie chandeliers such as those that now hang in Bristol Cathedral and the Royal Foundation

of St Katharine (see Early Forms). Yet it is probably the most successful and long-lived of all chandelier forms.

A pair of brass chandeliers that may offer a clue to the origins of the Dutch style hangs today in Hardwick Hall in Derbyshire, England, the home in the sixteenth century of the redoubtable Bess of Hardwick. Born in old Hardwick Hall in 1527, she died in the new hall in 1608. Having had four husbands, including the Earl of Shrewsbury, sometime gaoler to Mary Queen of Scots, in her later years Bess embarked on a huge programme of building at Hardwick. There she created a Renaissance palace with magnificent glazed windows, which earned it the popular soubriquet: "Hardwick Hall, more glass than wall". Furnishings of appropriate magnificence and luxury were imported, including the chandeliers. Believed to be of Flemish or possibly German manufacture, they are first mentioned in an inventory of 1601.

Each of the brass chandeliers at Hardwick has a central baluster, similar to the turned wood shapes seen in early American wood-and-wire examples. Two tiers of arms are attached to collars encircling protuberances on the baluster, which at that point become more pronounced, like flattened ovals. Each arm curls round into a decorative medallion at the baluster end, and extends outward almost horizontally before terminating in an elegant upturn to the drip pan and candle nozzle. Interestingly, the baluster end of each arm also features small straight spokes of brass radiating out from the medallion. These look like runnels through which the molten brass would have run when the arms were being moulded, which would normally be filed away during finishing. Instead they have been retained, perhaps for decorative purposes, perhaps for structural reasons. Whatever the case, there is none of the swooping downward curve of the arms that is so familiar from the typical Dutch form, and no pronounced globe on the stem. What was the relationship between the Dutch form and the elements we see at Hardwick?

The simplest theory is probably the best. Besides being a device for increasing reflectivity, the globe was also designed to endow the chandelier with

Above: *A brass chandelier, believed to be of seventeenth-century Dutch manufacture, hanging from the steeply vaulted stone ceiling of the Dining Room at Lindisfarne Castle in Northumbria.*

Left: *The Oak Staircase of Temple Newsam, Leeds, is generously lit by a pair of Dutch-style brass chandeliers, probably made by Thomas Elsley of London, hung one from the other. The upper one originally hung in the dining room; its companion was ordered in 1894, when work began on the staircase, and both were hung in 1897, when it was completed. A similar arrangement may be seen at The Argory in Northern Ireland (see p. 45).*

Left: *A charming golden chandelier, actually carved and gilded wood with gilded metal arms, in the Library of Berrington Hall, Herefordshire, built in the late eighteenth century. The chandelier, of unknown date, was brought here from Winnstay in Denbeighshire by the first Lord Cawley, who had it converted to electricity as part of a major refurbishment in 1900-6.*

Right: *The light shed by this impressive pair of chandeliers is supplemented by more candles in brass wall sconces of a similar design, as well as by those in candlesticks on the table.*

a centralizing force, a sufficient weight to keep it hanging straight and prevent it from swinging. Even if they were from the same mould, chandelier arms made by hand were not necessarily of identical weight. Without this central weight to balance it, therefore, the chandelier ran the possibility of tipping slightly to one side or the other, so potentially risking a practical as well as an aesthetic disaster. The arms were curved in order to bring the candles down to the level of the globe and so maximize the amount of light reflected in it. It is also possible that over time the arms became further bent by the attentions of servants, part of whose job was repeatedly to force candles down into the nozzles while holding the chandelier steady. This action was bound to exert a degree of leverage on the arms every time the chandelier was used: contemporary paintings almost invariably show chandeliers in daylight hours empty of candles, since these were a valuable commodity to be locked away when not needed. It is also possible that the arms started to droop slightly over time. Early brass tended to be low in zinc, making it less yellow and rather softer than the metal we know today. While this had the advantage of making it easier to work, it might also be the cause of a degree of droop in the arms. It also contained more impurities than modern brass, which made it less highly reflective when polished,

because of tiny pieces of grit on the surface, and less strong because of interruptions to the body of the brass.

Following the widespread destruction of brass chandeliers during the Reformation, they continued to be made for the cathedrals and churches, nonconformist chapels and meeting houses of Europe, and later similar locations in America. The style adopted was invariably the Dutch form, though over time variations appeared, including moving the arms onto the stem and later onto the globe itself.

The churches and cathedrals of England alone offer an astonishing variety of designs, with barely two the same. They were frequently engraved with the maker's name, sometimes accompanied by an edifying text. The chandelier in the nave of St Mary's Church, Totnes, Devon, for example, bears the verse: "Thy word is a lantern to my feet and a light unto my paths". Presented to the church in 1701 (chandeliers were a popular gift, to the greater glory not only of God and the church, but also of the donor), this example has the added charm of being surmounted by a carved oak finial in the form of a dove.

The finial was the chandelier-maker's final flourish, and an opportunity to indulge in decorative forms other than the curls and knops

incorporated into the structural members. The figure of the dove offered the advantage of combining a charming form with symbolic resonance. Not only did it represent the Holy Spirit, but it also played a key practical role in the tale of Noah. Its attitude also provides clues as to the geographical origins of the chandelier. A dove with its wings open, as on the example at St Mary's, probably indicated work from London. With its wings closed and its body smooth rather than feathered, it would have signified a Bristol origin. Other popular motifs for finials were a bishop's mitre, in the Church of England at least, and flames. Additional decoration, in the form of curlicues, hearts, crowns, flowers, or cherubs, was sometimes applied to the arms and between them, as well as between the tiers of branches.

The New World saw the arrival of many Dutch adventurers (New York was of course New Amsterdam until its capture by the British), and – with brass not yet readily available locally – subsequent generations of wealthy settlers continued to import chandeliers from Holland. These remained rare, however, and were most often used in public buildings. Williamsburg in Virginia, the capital of the British colonial government in the eighteenth century, now restored as a national monument, has several examples. The Long Gallery

Far left: *This chandelier (reflected in the mirror behind) lights the Venendaal House, an old canalside residence in Amsterdam, the Netherlands. The underlying structure supporting spectacular crystal chandeliers such as the ones on these pages is often of brass, an eminently workable material which was then frequently gilded.*

Left: *This fabulous gilt and crystal chandelier is Swedish, made in Stockholm by R.F. Lindroth to a design by the highly influential French early nineteenth-century architects Percier and Fontaine.*

of Independence Hall in Philadelphia, meanwhile, boasts an impressive row of them. Only one of these is original, however, the others being reproductions by one of the many companies who produce impressive copies and reinterpretations of historic chandeliers in the USA today.

Pioneering households could not afford brass chandeliers of this type, but they might improvise something similar. A tin chandelier now in the Cooper Union Museum, consisting of four arms radiating from a central plate on which stands a coloured glass ball, is virtually a unique survivor of its kind from this period. The ball serves the same purpose as the brass globe swelling from the central baluster of a Dutch chandelier, reflecting the candlelight and refracting it around the room as it bounces off the ball's curved surface.

Following the destruction that accompanied the Reformation, the next disaster to befall the brass chandeliers of Europe and America was the arrival in the nineteenth century of gas lighting, rapidly followed by electricity. Many chandeliers hanging in churches and places of worship were destroyed to make way for the new technology. Others eventually found their way into private

Left: *The chandelier lighting the Arab Hall at Leighton House in Kensington, the astonishing London home of the eminent Victorian artist Frederic Lord Leighton. Inspired by the banqueting room at the Moorish palace at La Zisa, a Moorish palace in Palermo, the Arab Hall was added to the house in 1877.*

Right: *A glittering chandelier of elaborately worked glass and metal hanging in a rococo Venetian salon.*

homes, where brass chandeliers in one form or another managed to retain their popularity. Indeed, they continued to be manufactured for wealthy customers. Grand European houses might have several brass chandeliers, which tended to remain true to historic forms but varied in their detail or use.

In the Great Hall of Temple Newsam, near Leeds in Yorkshire, founded in 1500 and extended and redecorated many times thereafter, hangs a massive two-tier chandelier, with twelve branches slotting into a collar between the two globes of the central baluster. Known as the Cheltenham Chandelier, this was made in 1738 by John Giles, later Master of the Founders' Company of the City of London, and hung in St Mary's Parish Church, Cheltenham, for a mere hundred years before it was removed by the churchwardens in order to make way for gas lighting (ironically, it was subsequently converted to run on gas power). After languishing in a crate, this "quantity of old metal formerly a chandelier" (suggesting it had been dismantled) passed through a number of hands including Colonel J.C.E. Harding Rolls, of Rolls-Royce fame. Finally, in 1964, it was bought for Temple Newsam,

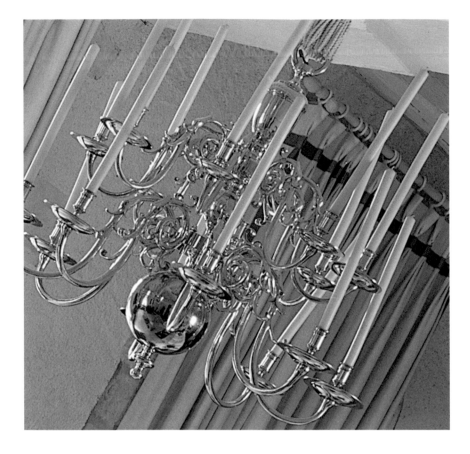

where it now hangs in a suitably magnificent setting. Many other fine brass chandeliers were not so lucky and disappeared without trace.

The spacious dining room at Temple Newsam houses a surprisingly small but unusually pretty brass chandelier. Designed by G.F. Bodley and made by Watts & Co. of London in 1877, it takes the familiar Dutch style of brass chandelier and turns it into something floral and decorative. The globe is cut in a decorative pattern to make a ball of tracery, and is also engraved with designs of Byzantine inspiration. The arms are attached in the familiar two-tier arrangement, six above and eight below, but the shaft is decorated in novel fashion with brass flowers. The effect is both surprising and charming.

The two-storey well of the huge oak main stair at Temple Newsam is lit by not one but two brass chandeliers, the lower one being suspended from its neighbour above. The idea of hanging one brass chandelier from another in an exceptionally tall, narrow space such as this is quite brilliant, but rarely seen. On a practical level, one large chandelier would be too bulky widthways, and would not provide so good a spread of light vertically as two. Naturally, the top chandelier must be sufficiently strong to take the weight not only of the lower chandelier but also of the chain from which it hangs. At Temple Newsam, the upper chandelier is substantial, with three tiers of six arms, while the lower one is smaller, with just two tiers also of six arms. The upper chandelier hung in the dining room until its companion piece was ordered from the same

manufacturer, probably Thomas Elsley of London, in 1894, after which they were hung in tandem as seen today.

The Great Hall and dining room chandeliers at Temple Newsam raise the interesting question of scale. According to one formula for calculating the appropriate size of chandelier for any given room, you should add the dimensions of a space in feet (10ft + 8ft for example), and the result represents the diameter in inches of a suitable light fitting (in this case 18 inches). Such guidelines may have their uses, but the Great Hall stands as a reminder that the human eye is unequalled as an instrument for making such calculations. Monumental as it is, the Cheltenham Chandelier is nevertheless too small according to the above formula. In other settings, a chandelier that is too big according to the same criteria may none the less provide just the desired degree of dramatic impact. The pretty brass chandelier in the dining room at Temple Newsam, meanwhile, seems much too small for the room at first glance. But it has been hung with great skill, suspended low over the table from the soaring ceiling. This creates two interesting effects. Firstly, the detail on the chandelier, which would be lost if it hung much higher, is clearly revealed. Secondly, the atmosphere surrounding the table is one of great intimacy: after dark, it becomes an oasis of warmth

Above left: *This handsome brass, antique patina gold and crystal chandelier was made in 1998 – almost entirely by hand – for the Ritz Carlton Hotel in Dubai by the prestigious Czech firm of Preciosa Lustry (established in 1724).*

Above right: *A fine example of the classic Dutch style of chandelier, with arms curling down around a heavy brass ball, the weight of which keeps the fitting level and helps to prevent it from swinging.*

Left: *The fascinating small brass chandelier that hangs over the dining table at Temple Newsam, Leeds, in classic Dutch style, embellished with flowers and leaves and a ball which is both pierced and decorated. The house is open to the public and contains a fine collection of chandeliers.*

Left: *A charming metal chandelier in the Hamburg home of fashion stylist Sybille Gerhardt, whose decorating style combines old flea market finds with metal furniture and pieces by contemporary designers.*

Below left: *The spacious arrangement of the arms of this old brass chandelier complement the airy, pared-down look of the room's contemporary decor.*

Right: *Such is the appeal of chandeliers in the twenty-first century that many high street retailers now include them in their lighting ranges. This six-light example, based on a French cage design and 70cm (2¼ ft) high, is the Marlow from Laura Ashley, with matching wall lights also available.*

and light, lapped by the mysterious darkness of the corners of this large room. A much larger chandelier would be impressive here, but possibly intimidating. We are now so used to the harsh brightness of electric light flooding every nook and cranny, moreover, that we tend to overlook the romantic qualities of darkness and shadow. Pools of useful but atmospheric light can be created within a shadowy room, and in a dining room there is no better way of doing this than by hanging a chandelier over the table. The dining room at Temple Newsam also serves as a useful reminder that chandeliers are often hung too high: as a general rule, the bottom should be not much above head height. Over a dining table, a chandelier may be hung lower still, as long as it does not impede the diners' view of each other.

Production of Dutch-style brass chandeliers dwindled gradually after the late nineteenth century, though they still managed to retain some interest in the face of other more "modern" styles. Even at the height of the Modern Movement's influence, they continued to be made and promoted. In 1952, for instance, W.J. Stokvis ran a shop at 118–20 Wardour Street in London and a workshop at Arnhem in Holland for the manufacture of "Light Fittings: replicas of the XVIIth century". Ready-fitted for electricity, these could be bought en suite with matching wall brackets. In order to convince clients of the authenticity of the chandeliers' pedigree, the catalogue was punctuated with

illustrations of seventeenth-century Dutch interiors, complete with similar lighting devices, by artists such as Gerard Terborch and Gabriel Metsu.

The advent of widely available gas lighting in the nineteenth century, when crystal chandeliers were otherwise the most fashionable and popular choice in homes across the western world, restored brass to its former prominence, this time in the manufacture of gasoliers. This attractive and useful material for making such a variety of appealing lighting appliances had never completely fallen out of use, however. Between the mid-eighteenth century and the early twentieth, many different types of lighting fuel were tried, including lard oil and kerosene (paraffin), with varying degrees of popularity and success. Of the numerous systems invented with the aim of achieving bright artificial light that was affordable, efficient, and clean, the Argand lamp was among the cleverest and most successful.

In 1784, the Swiss scientist Aimé Argand invented a system for enhancing a flame powered by colza oil (made from rape seed) with a supply of oxygen both up the middle of the wick and also around the outside of the flame. The result was astonishing. The light was unforgivingly bright and the flame burned cleanly on account of its great heat. Quickly copied in France and England, the Argand lamp was introduced to America by Thomas Jefferson, and by the advent of the nineteenth century Argand lamps and chandeliers – the Argand Versoix Pattern Book shows various designs of japanned metal decorated with surface patterns and strings of crystal beads and drops – were routinely to be found in the homes of wealthy Americans.

In its early years, gas was more popular for civic lighting than for domestic use, for which it was considered too bright and too hot. By the 1840s, however, gasoliers were to be found in many homes, especially in new buildings with gas piping installed in walls and ceilings as part of the construction process, and nowhere more so than in the United States. Kerosene was also hugely popular in America: the Sears, Roebuck & Co. catalogue of 1897, for instance, included several pages of advertisements for kerosene chandeliers. Then, of course, came the advent of electric light. The resulting choice in lighting systems, with no one type seeming to achieve pre-eminence, gave rise

Left: *Brass chandeliers hanging in the Great Hall at Cotehele, Cornwall. In fact only two of the chandeliers are original, the third being a late twentieth-century copy by Trelawny Jago of Plympton. For reasons that remain mysterious, the third chandelier from the original set was sent by the Edgcumbe family to another of their homes, at Mount Edgcumbe. Believed until recently to be of mid-eighteenth-century manufacture, the chandeliers have now been re-dated on stylistic grounds to the mid- to late-nineteenth century by the National Trust's lighting expert, Dr Maureen Dillon.*

Above: *The handsome Double Orb chandelier from McCloud Lighting in England. Kevin McCloud is a designer, writer, and broadcaster who manufactures fine contemporary lighting in a variety of styles, including this reinterpretation of the classic Dutch ball with curving arms.*

Right: *The massed arms and glass globes of this brass chandelier in the Château de Groussay, near Versailles, are busy and impressive, giving an impression of weighty solidity.*

Far right: *Gracie Chandelier by McCloud Lighting, an unusual contemporary design featuring porcelain shades for the lights, borne on simple, slender arms.*

to a wide variety of chandelier forms, as well as to some interesting brass and glass hybrids. The gasolier-electrolier, with gas jets pointing upward and electric bulbs pointing downward, represented the ultimate in style and practicality. Gas could be used to supplement the electric power when more light was needed or in an emergency, and with fittings pointing both up and down, the whole room was lit effectively.

Some chandeliers still took traditional forms, but with a structure formed from hollow brass rods which allowed the owner the choice of using candles or powering the fitting with gas. One example, dating from about 1845 and now in a private collection in Mississippi, has the astonishing addition of a glass vase at its centre, intended to hold a bouquet of flowers. In America at least, "bouquet chandeliers" such as this were not as rare as might be imagined.

Gasoliers varied in form from quite simple, elegant shapes with curving arms attached to a central ball, a design clearly related to earlier brass chandeliers, to flamboyant and heavily decorated Victorian creations, incorporating motifs such as birds, gryphons, angels, and flowers in a profusion of ornamentation. Glass shades for the flames were often decorated with engraved or coloured patterns. Among the best-known American manufacturers

of gasoliers and other lighting fittings was Cornelius and Company, whose work can still be seen in buildings as far apart as the Edmondston-Alston House in Charleston, South Carolina, and the Philadelphia Athenaeum, lit by gas from 1847 to 1923, when electric lighting took over.

We now take the pre-eminence of electricity for granted, but early supplies were feared to be unreliable and potentially harmful. An advertisement for the Brascolite brand of electric pendant light fittings reassured its customers that the product was "Best Suited to Eye Health and Comfort – Because the design is scientifically correct. The glass bowl softens and diffuses the lamp rays and disposes of glare". The world's first power station producing electricity for lighting and other purposes was opened in 1880 at Holborn Viaduct in London, to be followed two years later by the Pearl Street power station in New York. Yet gasoliers and gas lamps remained in use and manufacture well into the early twentieth century.

Brass has a close cousin in bronze, an alloy of copper and tin, which was and is still used for making chandeliers (often as a base for a final gilded finish). Though its warm colour is pleasing, its tone is browner and generally less distinctive and glamorous than that of brass, and it has never been as widely used.

Right: *The massive brass Cheltenham Chandelier in the Great Hall of Temple Newsam, Leeds, was made in 1738 by John Giles, later Master of the Founders' Company in the City of London. After hanging in its original location in St Mary's Parish Church, Cheltenham, for a mere hundred years, it was ignominiously removed and deposited in a crate by the churchwardens to make way for gas lighting. Ironically, a later owner altered it to be powered by gas.*

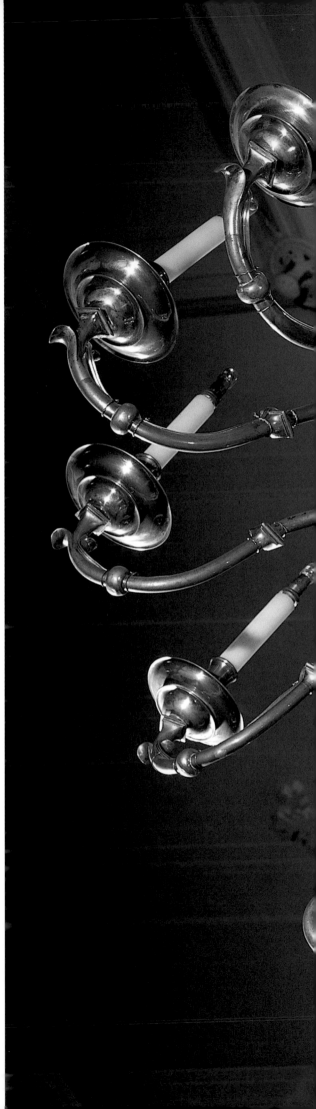

VENETIAN GLASS

After the masculine seriousness and handsome good looks

of iron, wood, and brass chandeliers, the delightfully delicate

froth and femininity of their Venetian cousins comes as

agreeably light relief. Curvy, flirtatious, and flowery,

Venetian glass chandeliers are above all pretty, even if

the business of making them has been a matter of high

seriousness for centuries.

Previous page left:
An impressive Venetian chandelier hanging in Lacock Abbey, Wiltshire (owned by the National Trust and open to the public), thought possibly to be constructed from parts of two incomplete or damaged Venetian chandeliers.

Previous page right:
A detail of the Palladio glass chandelier, made by the Vetraria de Majo glassmakers on Murano, Venice.

Left: *An elegantly ornate glass chandelier hangs in an equally opulent setting – but a fine chandelier will look glamorous in virtually any surroundings.*

Right and below right: *Two modern chandeliers, both classic in form, show how the traditional style of Venetian chandelier that first appeared around 1700 is still alive and popular today, effortlessly complementing even the most minimalist of settings.*

These breathtaking "confections in glass" are a sheer delight to the eye: a characteristically elaborate Venetian chandelier might have two tiers of lights, the lower with a dozen curved arms, the upper with eight or ten. Each is formed from pieces of clear glass, many twisted into decorative shapes, and others incorporating or edged with coloured glass in glowing green, turquoise, blue, purple, or red. The stem is encased in balusters and bulbous glass shapes, also decorated and tinted. But most delightful of all is the veritable garden of brilliantly coloured glass flowers crowding the stem and arms. From the lowest point there dangles a striped and coloured bauble (with smaller versions hanging on rings from the lowest point of each arm), while more flowers and other decorative forms twine up from above the top tier of lights to the very ceiling. Were you to take the chandelier apart, for the purposes of cleaning or restoration, you would find between one and two hundred separately made pieces, depending on its size. The effect produced by a Venetian chandelier on this scale is almost overwhelming. And despite its considerable mass and highly complex construction, it nevertheless contrives to give an impression of airy weightlessness.

Not all Venetian chandeliers are so huge or elaborate, however. While the example described above would require a large, lofty room or broad stairwell in which to hang, others are much simpler, made from clear glass and considerably more modest in scale. And as the same high level of skill and

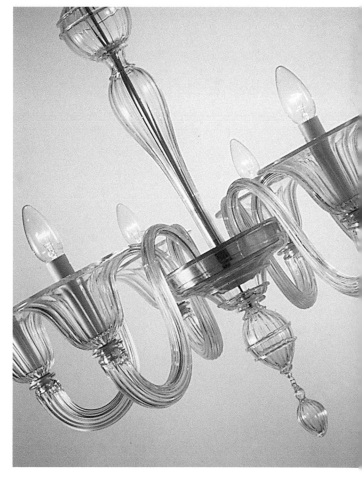

artistry are deployed by the glassblower in the formation of their pieces, they have a similarly delightful presence. Lying somewhere between these two types is the kind of chandelier found in so many Venetian homes: charmingly elegant in form, employing not more than one or two colours, and needing only a moderately high ceiling from which to hang comfortably. Still made in Venice today, these chandeliers are probably among the best-known products of the Venetian glassmaking industry, as well as being the latest in a tradition that goes back hundreds of years.

While the history of glassmaking in Venice goes back well over a millennium and is central to this great trading city's history, it was only in around the year 1700 that these skills began to be applied to the creation of chandeliers. At the same time, northern Europe and north America saw the emergence of a parallel, equally elegant but much more sharply defined development in the form of glass chandeliers, following the discovery in 1676 by George Ravenscroft of London of lead crystal (see Eighteenth and Nineteenth Century Elegance).

The history of Venetian chandeliers is inextricably bound up with the history of Venetian glass, and the story of glass production is as romantic and dramatic as the city's geography and long history. Glassmaking had been an important industry in Venice for centuries by the time the Venetian form of chandelier emerged around 1700. The Venetian glassblowers' guild was established as early as 1224, with the aim of rediscovering the skills of the glassmakers of ancient Rome and of creating pieces as fine as theirs. By 1292, when the city's glass furnaces were moved from the main islands in the lagoon to the smaller and less central island of Murano, Venetian glassmaking was a sophisticated and highly regarded industry. Security was one factor behind this famous move, and the other was the potentially catastrophic fire risk posed to the city's wooden structures by the glass furnaces.

In the fifteenth century, the Venetian Republic was at the height of its power and influence. As trade flowed west from Constantinople and the Far East, Venice grew rich and mighty, and her citizens wanted only the best. This the glassmakers on Murano were uniquely well qualified to provide. They excelled at creating finely wrought objects of beauty and necessity for Venetian citizens,

as well as sought-after goods for traders, who from the early fourteenth century exchanged them for valuable spices and silks. Their traditional skills in making drinking vessels, beads, and window glass were further enhanced by the arrival of fugitive Byzantine glassworkers, who brought with them the secrets of the Islamic glassmaking tradition. Venetian glassmakers enjoyed considerable privileges. Men were permitted to wear swords, and women were allowed to marry into the Venetian aristocracy without any threat to the nobility of their lineage. But there were also special penalties for glassmakers and their families if they were found to have given away any of the trade's jealously guarded secrets. The glassmakers of Murano were forbidden under pain of death to leave the Republic or under any circumstances to reveal any details about the production of Venetian glass. Surprisingly, even these measures failed to act as a watertight deterrent, and some glassmakers did escape and set up their own workshops elsewhere in Europe, where their skills were eagerly welcomed and their goods highly prized. Across Europe, glass was made following the *façon de Venise*, making it difficult now to establish a Venetian provenance with any certainty.

It was also in the fifteenth century that a great rediscovery was made. The art of producing clear glass by adding manganese dioxide had been lost in the Dark Ages. Now the Venetian glassmakers found that the addition of manganese dioxide to the basic silica resulted in a glass that was completely clear. Indeed, it was as clear as the crystal that the glassmakers had for years been striving to imitate. Hence it was known as cristallo. The properties of this glass form the basis for the intricate, highly decorative, and lavishly embellished forms of Venetian glass, which found one of its finest expressions in the production of chandeliers.

Venetian chandeliers typically feature intricate arabesques of leaves and flowers, with fine twists and turns created by the incorporation of threads of coloured glass. All this was made possible by the fact that the cristallo with which the glass-workers on Murano were working was soda glass, with its alkaline content provided by soda ash rather than potash, like the glass made in ancient Rome and Egypt. As it also contains a small quantity of lime it is sometimes known as soda-lime glass. Bohemian and central European glass, by contrast, contained potash, while English and American crystal contained lead.

Above: *Exquisite examples of locally made glass chandeliers, incorporating the finest traditions of Venetian glassmaking, light the Hotel Cipriani in Venice.*

Above left: *A magnificent Venetian chandelier in a modern setting on a suitably grand scale. The architectural simplicity and fine materials of the hall and gallery offset the intricate detail of the glasswork.*

Right: *Novecento,
created in 1996 by
Orlano Navareno, is a bold
demonstration of the way
in which the glassmakers
of Murano are developing
new idioms for their art.
This uncompromisingly
modern piece is from
Vetraria de Majo.*

The overall proportions of Venetian soda glass are roughly sixty per cent silica to twenty-five per cent soda and fifteen per cent lime (with traces of other matter such as impurities and manganese). One of the most outstanding qualities of soda glass is its lightness. Another is that when heated it remains plastic, or soft and workable, for longer than lead crystal. A visit to a Murano glass factory reveals exactly how long a craftsman takes to twist and shape a frond for a chandelier, using his blow rod and pincers – as long as he likes, it seems, so smooth and unhurried are his actions. This owes a great deal to skill, of course – you may be watching a craftsman with forty years' experience – but the nature of the glass is also of fundamental importance. Soda glass is also different from lead crystal in that it has no resonance (it does not "ring" when you tap it) and its brittleness makes it unsuitable for cutting or engraving. Unlike lead-crystal chandeliers, which gain sparkle from their cut facets, especially the drops, the play of light on a Venetian glass chandelier is a function of its decoration and form. Once blown, pincered, twisted, and cooled, the arms and leaves of Venetian work have taken on their final, unchanging appearance.

One of the earliest examples of a Venetian glass chandelier is to be found not in Venice, but at Rosenborg Castle in Copenhagen. In 1709, Frederick

Above: *Organicosmo (1998)*
by Maria Grazin Rosin is
another brilliantly coloured
testament to the ability
of Venetian glassmakers
to adapt centuries-old
traditions and skills
to contemporary tastes.

IV of Denmark travelled to Venice and is believed to have visited Murano. By 1718, a chandelier specifically referred to as "Italian" had appeared in the palace inventory, along with a quantity of other fine Venetian glassware. The chandelier still hangs in the palace, a fine souvenir of the king's Italian travels.

The great historic palazzi along the Grand Canal in Venice have their grand reception rooms on the piano nobile, raised above the ground floor. Until quite recently, there were many evenings when you could travel the length of the canal at dusk by vaporetto, watching the magnificent eighteenth- and nineteenth-century chandeliers being lit up as guests arrived for parties and artistic events. From the level of the canal below, the water-borne traveller enjoys an uninterrupted view of the ceilings of these magnificent rooms and their dazzling chandeliers, sparkling with light. Nowadays, Venetian residents lament the fact that so many of the palazzi have been bought by big corporations, banks, and businesses, who use these rooms and light up the chandeliers only on rare occasions. Consequently, the Grand Canal at night is dark and deadened: some of the life goes out of Venice, they say, when the chandeliers are not lit.

The fall of the Venetian Republic in 1797 was followed by occupation by the armies of Napoleon, who caused widespread devastation in the city, on

Left: *The charmingly coloured red and blue glass detail, and the fine twisting and pincering of the work, are revealed in this close-up of a Venetian chandelier currently hanging in a Paris apartment.*

Left: *With its delicate, jewel-like colours and superb workmanship, this spectacular new Venetian chandelier from Barovier & Toso on Murano maintains the standards and techniques of the highest classic tradition.*

Right: *Tulip-shaped flowers in crimson-coloured glass adorn a voluptuous glass chandelier hanging in a modern Turkish interior designed by Ruya Mocan.*

Murano as elsewhere. Most of the glassworks closed and the old techniques and skills were all but lost. Not only did the occupation almost put an end to the production of fine glass, but also, inevitably, many of the skilled craftsmen and their families moved abroad to find work. This exodus of expertise and experience, combined with the severe tax duties imposed on both raw materials and finished products by the Austrians, who succeeded the Napoleonic occupiers of the city-state, nearly signalled the end of a great tradition.

The story of one Muranese manufacturer of chandeliers, Fratelli Toso (the Toso brothers), serves to illustrate the means by which the Venetian glassmaking tradition survived this terrible period in its history. Pietro Toso remained in Venice throughout the occupation. In 1848, his six sons, Ferdinando, Carlo, Liberato, Angelo, Giovanni, and Gregorio, found premises in what had once been the Scuola Grande di S. Giovanni dei Battuti, and set themselves up in business. At first, their production was of typically poor quality, for the industry on Murano generally was at a low ebb. Demand, such as it was, came largely from the Carmelite friars, who needed glass containers for the goods they manufactured, such as lemon balm and pharmaceutical oils and

tinctures. Some domestic items were also produced, but overall the glass from this period was utilitarian and mundane. It was as if the will and the skill of making fine glass had been stamped out by Napoleon and the Austrian invaders.

In the mid-nineteenth century, however, a quiet revolution occurred in which the Toso brothers played a part. Three men in particular are credited with bringing about the resurgence in Venetian glassmaking: Dr Antonio Salviati, a lawyer turned glassmaking businessman, Antonio Colleoni, mayor of Murano, and Abbot Vincenzo Zanetti. It was Zanetti who visited Gregorio Toso to suggest that he allow his glassmakers to train in the making of fine handmade glass in the evenings, when the day's routine work was done. Colleoni and Zanetti, meanwhile, began gathering together documents and examples of antique glass in order to form a study collection from which the Toso brothers and other glassmakers could learn.

By 9 April 1860, a Fratelli Toso craftsman, Guiseppe Gaggio, had completed a stupendous glass chandelier, a tribute to the renewal of the Venetian glassmaking industry. According to Bartolomeo Cecchetti (quoted by A. Gasparetto in *Vetri di Murano*, 1960), it was 2.83m (9¼ft) tall and 1.83m (6ft) in diameter, and contained no fewer than 1,700 separate glass pieces. By 1864, just a decade after Fratelli Toso was founded, the company was able to present to the newly opened museum of glass on Murano (based on Colleoni and Zanetti's study collection) a fabulous chandelier in the true Venetian tradition. Whether or not this was the same Gaggio creation is unclear. The chandelier still hangs in the Museo Vetrario, occupying pride of place in the Grand Salon. Fratelli Toso, meanwhile, credited themselves with rescuing the art of glass in Venice, and in 1879 opened a shop in the heart of Venice, on the prestigious Rialto Bridge over the Grand Canal.

In the nineteenth century, two foreign powers, Britain and the United States, also made a substantial contribution to the renaissance of Venetian glass. To set up his first glassmaking business, the former lawyer Dr Antonio Salviati turned for funds to investors he knew through their admiration of Venetian glass, including the British Member of Parliament Sir Austen Henry Layard. British cognoscenti particularly appreciated the twists and turns, the frivolous fantasies,

the dragons, dolphins, serpents, and extravagant blossoms of Venetian glassware. Schooled by the writings of the art critic John Ruskin, designer, craftsman, and socialist critic William Morris, and other members of the Arts and Crafts Movement, they admired objects that were handmade and the product of one man's craftsmanship. In *The Stones of Venice* (1851-3), Ruskin praised Venetian glass and deplored the products of "barbarous" cut glass (of the type celebrated in the next chapter), because they could only be made joylessly with the aid of machinery. Despite such adulation, Venetian craftsmen remained anonymous. We know few of the names of those responsible for the design or creation of any individual item of traditional glassware or chandelier.

Wealthy Americans, meanwhile, travelled around Europe on a sort of nineteenth-century Grand Tour, broadening their culture and education and drinking in the sights of the great cities. As most tourists do, they fell in love with Venice. They also bought up the output of the revived Venetian glassworks with enthusiasm, to the extent that almost eighty per cent of the glass produced in the years before World War I is believed to have been exported to the United States. A particular shade of red glass was even dubbed *rosso americano* in homage to its popularity with the Americans. In 1881, James Jackson Jarves, son of a glass magnate, gave a substantial collection of fine Venetian glass to the recently opened Metropolitan Museum of Art in New York, where it can still be seen and enjoyed by the public. Though it contains no chandeliers, it is a powerful testimony to the popularity of Venetian glass in the US, and hence of the importance of the American contribution to the revival of the Venetian glass

Left: *Coiled fronds and curlicues unfurl like ferns in this unusual gilded glass chandelier.*

Right: *This traditional chandelier embodies all the purity of the Venetian tradition, which at its best has a uniquely ethereal quality. Praising the authentic craftsmanship of Venetian glass, Ruskin deplored what he described as the barbarousness of cut glass.*

industry. The Corning Museum has an exquisite glass chandelier made by Salviati & Co., with six arms and turquoise flowers and edging, as well as a number of red and white carnations and even glass chains.

In the twentieth century, the upheavals of two world wars represented temporary disasters for Venetian glass production, as for the manufacture of other luxury items. During World War I, Venice and the rest of united Italy were at war with Austria once again. As Austro-German shells rained over the border, the city found itself in the front line. In 1917, the glassworks of leading companies such as Fratelli Toso, Artisti Barovier, and Andrea Rioda were transferred from Murano to Livorno on the mainland. But in the 1920s and again in the later 1940s, the production of fine glass including chandeliers enjoyed periods of prosperity once more, thanks largely to American interest and purchasing power.

Following many further internal upheavals, the Toso company is still in business, under its new name, Antica Vetreria Fratelli Toso. Still managed by members of the Toso family, it is based on the Fondamenta Colleoni on Murano, and examples of its fine work can be seen in museums and galleries across the world, including the Louvre in Paris and the Corning Museum of Glass in New York. If you choose a Fratelli Toso traditional chandelier (they also design and make contemporary lighting), you are buying not merely a superb light fitting but also a piece of Venetian glassmaking history.

Left: *A pretty metal chandelier festooned with glass ornaments.*

Right: *Though small, this French metal chandelier achieves maximum impact through the addition of clear and blue glass tear-drops.*

A traditional Venetian chandelier made by one of Murano's prestigious manufacturers such as Barovier and Toso or Venini is equally comfortable in a Venetian palazzo as in a modern home because the designs have remained virtually unaffected by the passage of the centuries. In 1955, David Lean made the Hollywood classic, *Summertime*, starring Katharine Hepburn as American spinster Jane Hudson, seeking love in Venice. In an emotional scene at her hotel, she has an argument with the man she has fallen in love with, an antique dealer, over the provenance of a piece of glass he has sold to her. He explains to Jane that in the history of Venetian glass, "the same design is used over and over again. Your goblet is eighteenth century". This is a worthwhile point, since a modern Venetian chandelier of traditional form is almost indistinguishable on stylistic grounds from one made in the eighteenth or nineteenth centuries.

The twentieth century, however, witnessed a new development – the emergence of art glass on Murano. For the first time women have assumed a prominent place in Venetian glassmaking, and pieces are attributed to individuals as well as to manufacturers. The products of this movement are mostly glass sculptures and vessels, with some jewellery. Given the strong sense of tradition on Murano (if only in order to flout it), it was inevitable, nevertheless, that a few chandeliers should feature among the new wave of Venetian glass. With their bold, bright colours and simple forms, these resemble on the one hand a new breed, and on the other a primitive, insect-like life form. They stand as proof, if proof were needed, that Venetian glass is a living, growing art form, as alive today as it was three or more centuries ago.

EIGHTEENTH AND NINETEENTH CENTURY ELEGANCE

European and American crystal chandeliers of the eighteenth and

nineteenth centuries arguably represent the apogee of the art of

chandelier-making. With their waterfalls of drops, shimmering and

twinkling in the light, these scintillating creations embody the ultimate

in chandelier design and technology. At one with the high ceilings and

fine proportions of the architecture of the period, crystal chandeliers

have a sophisticated elegance that is at once impressive and romantic.

Previous page left:
*Drops and pendants –
designed to tremble in
draughts and breezes –
reveal the glittering éclat
of crystal chandeliers.*

Previous page right:
*This detail of a crystal
chandelier illustrates
the sheer delicate beauty
of their form.*

Above left: *With their
tantalizing, trembling drops
and icicles, crystal
chandeliers play with light
in a way that we find
irresistible.*

Above right: *Pendant
drops and icicles add extra
sparkle and movement,
contributing to the effect
of a shimmering cascade
of light.*

Far right: *A crystal
chandelier will provide
an eye-catching focus
for virtually any interior,
whatever its size or style.
This example hangs in the
stately Villa Lita in Cuba.*

The first crystal chandeliers were literally carved out of rock, with each individual piece cut from a chunk of quartz and then hung from a metal frame, often finished with gilt or silver gilt. Not surprisingly, they cost a small fortune and were inevitably acquired only by the supremely wealthy few. These included Catherine de Medici, who died in 1589, and Cardinal Mazarin, chief minister of France from 1643, who reputedly hung his from silver chains. The few early rock-crystal chandeliers that survive, generally dating from the seventeenth and early eighteenth centuries, are to be found mostly in Europe. But America also has at least one from this period, bought in from Paris in the late twentieth century and now in the J. Paul Getty Museum in California.

Sweden has a number of surviving rock-crystal chandeliers, including one in the King's Hall in Skokloster, where it hangs from the jaws of a dragon on the ceiling, and another at Drottningsholms Slott. There are three seventeenth-century examples at Hampton Court Palace in England; the most charming of these, which hangs in the Queen's Audience Chamber, has a frame of silvered brass embellished with the forms of the lion and unicorn of the royal arms. The fate of one of the rock-crystal chandeliers in the Royal Collection at Hampton Court serves as a poignant and salutary reminder of the miraculous nature of the survival of any of these pieces into the twenty-first century. You would be forgiven for imagining that there could be no safer place for such a rare and fragile masterpiece than the King's Privy Chamber in this historic royal palace, in the expert care of specialized curators and conservators. But in

Above: *Crystal chandeliers can be just as much at home in an uncluttered contemporary interior as in an elaborately decorated space. The cool, grey tones of lead crystal lend themselves to a pale, muted style of interior decoration.*

Right: *Following their first appearance in the second half of the eighteenth century, crystal drops rapidly assumed a dazzling array of shapes and sizes.*

Far right: *Even the simplest metal chandelier is transformed with the addition of a mass of substantial, dangling drops.*

1986 a fire raged through Hampton Court, destroying many of its treasures. Not only did the ceiling of the Privy Chamber first of all collapse, smashing much of the chandelier on the floor, but the cold water from the firemen's hoses on the hot crystal then caused stress cracks in the surviving pieces. Amazingly, the chandelier now hangs in place again, restored and reconstructed by Martin Mortimer, the leading expert on these chandeliers, and his team at the famous British company Delomosne & Son Ltd.

Common elements in the shape and decoration of all these known rock-crystal chandeliers have encouraged Martin Mortimer to conclude that one style with similar features prevailed throughout Europe. This contrasts with the development of the later lead-crystal chandeliers (which were actually made of glass) of the eighteenth and nineteenth centuries, which alongside their similarities displayed marked national differences in style.

Most crystal chandeliers are not in fact made from rock crystal, but rather from a type of glass known as lead crystal. This was first made by an Englishman, George Ravenscroft, in about 1675 (the St Louis glass manufactory in France is believed to have discovered the method independently

Above: *As pretty as it is
flamboyant, this chandelier
finds an appropriately
dainty setting in the Rococo
Room of Kasteel vans
Gravenwezel near Antwerp,
Belgium, rebuilt in the
eighteenth century.*

Left: *A handsome
chandelier with a Regency
outline, with a hoop
sprouting short arms and
supporting a waterfall of
glass prisms, with strings of
drops rising up to a coronet.*

in 1781). A merchant in English and Venetian glass, Ravenscroft set up glass houses in and near London in the 1670s, where he experimented with various recipes for producing a clear, strong glass that resembled rock crystal but did not "crissle", a defect that caused small faults to appear within the glass. Potash caused crissling, but its presence was necessary to help the fusion during the manufacturing process of the various ingredients, mainly silica, in order to create clear glass. Bohemian glass production was similarly based on a potash "metal". Ravenscroft replaced some of the silica with lead oxide to produce lead crystal. Very few fragments of his glass, distinguished by the impression of a raven's head, survive: a mere twenty-five were known in 1968.

lead crystal has many valuable qualities, including its brilliance, the way that it disperses light, its wonderful clarity (Venetian glass, by comparison, is very slightly cloudy), and its softness. Less hard and brittle than Venetian glass, it is well suited to being cut into shapes and facets. Today, lead crystal must contain at least twenty-four per cent lead oxide before it can be called "half lead," and at least thirty per cent lead oxide to qualify as "full lead" or "cristal supérieur".

The practice of cutting the glass pieces used in chandeliers is believed to have originated with the manufacture not of glass vessels but of mirrors or looking glasses for walls. The first known mention of the word "schandelier" was in 1714, in an advertisement for the wares of John Gumley of London, whose primary trade was in gilt gesso, glass for carriage windows, and looking glasses. Many of the latter incorporated arms for carrying candles attached to the bottom of the frame, known as the apron. The glass of the mirror, meanwhile, was bevelled. The art of cutting these angled surfaces was subsequently applied – in what is possibly the first recorded application of glass-cutting techniques to three-dimensional objects – to the globes, dishes, and other glass pieces strung onto the central metal stem of the chandelier.

The first glass chandeliers are also the simplest, though simple styles remained in production for many years. In form, these early chandeliers bear a striking resemblance to the Dutch-style brass chandeliers, their arms curving down from a central stem with a bulbous globe, though on glass chandeliers the globe is usually set higher up the stem. Like the famous example in the chapel

Above: Even bathrooms can gain a touch of glamour from the addition of a chandelier: in this case a Laura Ashley gilt and crystal example in a setting combining elegance and restraint.

of Emmanuel College, Cambridge (given and probably made in 1732), early glass chandeliers had plain arms. By about 1740, however, their makers had begun to take pleasure both in the unique intrinsic qualities of the material and in the way that it reflects and refracts light. On both stem and arms, the cutting of extra facets into the glass served to multiply the number of surfaces off which the candlelight could ricochet. Rather than incising into the curved surface, however, craftsmen cut the sides of the arms into flat planes, notching angles at the corners where they met. An example from the early 1730s, now in the Winterthur Museum, Delaware, has plain arms, while a glass chandelier of strikingly similar design but made twenty years later, now hanging in Independence Hall, Philadelphia, has arms notched along their length to increase reflectivity.

Interestingly, the drip pan around each candle nozzle was also decorated, with a cut edge projecting prettily in points rather like a sweetmeat

dish. This finish was referred to as a "cornered brim". The "Van Dyck" cut denoted another type of decorated edge, reminiscent of the intricate "V"-edged pattern of lace collars worn by the sumptuously dressed subjects of portraits by that artist, including the ill-fated English king Charles I.

The next significant development in the design of glass chandeliers was the introduction in the second half of the eighteenth century of pendant drops. The addition of suspended pieces of glass accorded well with the lightness and elegance of neoclassicism, particularly as practised by the Adam brothers in their exquisite interiors, all extenuated lines and decorative intricacy. The addition of drops – of all shapes and sizes – to glass chandeliers added extra sparkle, created more movement (especially in the draughts that were then inescapable), and endowed the pieces with more glamour and allure. It also brought the crystal chandelier ever closer to the modern ideal of a magical cascade of shimmering light.

Above: Cascades of crystal drops, artfully arranged, transform two simple tiers of candles into something at once majestic and magical.

The design of drops encompasses an infinite variety. They may be round, in various sizes and with different patterns of faceting, or pear-shaped, with or without incisions. The most enticing might be star-shaped, either cut or (later) moulded in imitation of pieces of carved rock crystal, or they might be shaped like rosettes, crescents, or fleurs-de-lis. Later still, icicle drops appeared, cut into a huge variety of profiles – short, long, slim, and broad – all with the same basic stretched diamond shape. The catalogue for 1812 of the English maker Thomas Osler offers on a single page seven different sizes and styles of "spangles" (round faceted drops), six types of "chain drop" (pear-shaped with a pointed top), six types of "barley corn" (oval with pointed ends), and no fewer than twenty-six sizes and styles of icicle drop.

Increasingly, drops and other glass elements were bought in, often from Bohemia and other cheaper foreign sources, rather than being cut by the chandelier manufacturers themselves. The latter were then responsible for the design, assembly, and marketing of their wares. The famous William Parker (of whom more below) was unusual in apparently not buying cheaper drops from abroad, but preferring instead to make his own from genuine lead crystal, buying glass "blanks" from the nearby Whitefriars glassworks in London and having them cut in his own workshops. As far as we know, the designs for his chandeliers were his own.

In addition to drops, glass chandeliers seduced the eye with numerous other forms of decoration. They sprouted vertical spires of glass, sometimes placed between the candles and supported on an arm inserted for this exclusive purpose. Canopies in various shapes appeared on the upper half of the stem, sometimes more than one, their importance (and size) increasing as strings of drops appeared to festoon the chandeliers with necklaces of light. Attached at the top to a canopy, these described a graceful outward curve before being caught up at their lower extremity and attached to the arms. They were also draped between the arms. The candles themselves were shaded with tall glass cups (selected and purchased separately from the chandelier itself), which further increased the surface area from which light could reflect as well as protecting the flames from draughts. Sometimes, though rarely, astonishing

Above: *Small and delicate but with a touch of grandeur, this crystal chandelier presides over an imposing marble bath in a sixteenth-century Roman villa.*

Left: *Little is known about the magnificent and extraordinary lantern-cum-chandelier hanging in the stairwell of a private apartment block in Hong Kong, except that it is believed to be Bohemian crystal.*

glass swags were cut in their entirety from a solid piece of glass, as on the chandeliers at Uppark in Sussex. Dating from around 1775, these remarkable examples also provide the first known appearance of pear-shaped drops.

Other interesting variations include chandelier arms formed with a "double kick", and arms curved to different lengths and heights and then arranged in tiers, so that candles flicker at every level, dazzling the eye. This multilayered style of chandelier marks an intermediate stage between designs that came before and after. Before, the shaft up the middle of the chandelier was clearly seen, and the arms (which link the shaft architecturally and visually to the light sources) were distinct and not especially numerous. After, the shaft remains visible but is partly obscured behind a forest of arms, some supporting lights and others spires, with a multitude of drops and decorations adding to the distractions. Later still, in the Regency period, the underlying structure (consisting of either a stem or chains) vanished completely, with the design focusing on massed, regimented ranks of drops in a variety of shapes and sizes.

The undisputed world centre of lead-crystal chandeliers was London. Among the many well known makers here in the later part of the eighteenth

Left: *"Like light dissolved in star-showers"*: Shelley's description of waves breaking seems to capture the cool beauty of this glittering mass of cut and moulded crystal drops.

Far left: *Crystal beads strung onto a geometric net of wires, with large pendant drops attached, provide a grandiose tent and bag arrangement for a single large hoop. This chandelier hangs in the Château de Groussay, near Versailles.*

Above: *A similar hoop, tent, and bag profile may be seen in this example, but here the decoration consists of gracefully draped strings of beads culminating in a small waterfall.*

Above: *The sleek and understatedly elegant dining room of a Paris apartment gains not only a note of chic but also warmth and life from the light trapped like water in the crystal drops of a pretty chandelier.*

Right: *A glamorous Schonbek chandelier hung low over a simple kitchen table provides a lesson in the power of contrasts: remove it, and the room loses far more than merely a source of light.*

century, including Thomas Collet, Maydwell & Windle, Thomas Betts, John Blades, and Jerome Johnson, one in particular is outstanding. The reputation of William Parker of Fleet Street was based initially on a set of chandeliers he made for the Assembly Rooms in the fashionable spa town of Bath. Here, well-to-do families rented elegant terraced houses for the "season", spending their days taking the waters at the Roman baths or drinking it in the magnificent Assembly Rooms (opened in 1771), and by night attending glittering dances and receptions (again in the Assembly Rooms). Parker was originally commissioned to make only a few of the chandeliers, but when those made by his rival, Thomas Collet, developed an unfortunate tendency to drop their arms, he received a further contract to "provide five lustres for the Ball Room, the whole to contain two hundred candles, the fashion and ornaments to be left to Mr Parker, who is to deliver and put them up in ten weeks at the farthest for the sum of £500". One of the developments that emerged from this embarrassing episode was Parker's realization that if the arms were tapered, rather than being the same thickness all along, they would be lighter at the ends. This in turn would lessen the degree of leverage at the point where the arms joined the stem, so making it less of a weak spot. Tapering arms are also more delicate in appearance, thus contributing to the exceptional elegance of Parker's chandeliers.

The greatest and wealthiest in the land bought their chandeliers from William Parker. From 1782, the Duke of Devonshire purchased a range of lighting fixtures for his palatial home at Chatsworth in Derbyshire, and the Prince Regent bought chandeliers for his London home, Carlton House, at a cost of nearly £2,500, then a colossal sum. Later, the Prince Regent ordered a fifty-six-light chandelier for the Crimson Drawing Room at Carlton House. Installed in 1808, this sensational piece measured 4.2m (13¾ft) tall, and cost 1,000 guineas. Instead of one hoop with arms for candles it had three, with further tiers of drops above giving it the appearance of an inverted three-tier wedding cake. Contemporary illustrations of the interiors of Carlton House suggest chandeliers of massive proportions, soaring ceilingward and towering over the midget-like humans who people the rooms. A couple of decades later, some of these chandeliers were dismantled and altered, eventually finding homes in various

rooms at Buckingham Palace. In 1802-3, Parker joined forces with William Perry, another established designer and manufacturer of elegant chandeliers, to form the Parker and Perry company, which later still (1817) became Perry & Co. It survived into the age of Modernism, but finally closed in 1935.

In the early years of the nineteenth century an entirely new design of chandelier emerged, known as the Regency style. Long, elegant arms growing from a central stem gave way to shorter arms sprouting from a wide hoop of brass or bronze, gold-plated or gilded. High above was a coronet or canopy, much smaller in diameter than the hoop. From this countless strings of drops (growing larger as they descended) swung down to the hoop, producing the impression of a tent of light. Below the hoop hung either a bag of strings of drops (much shallower in depth than the height of the tent), or concentric circles of glass icicles that grew longer nearer the centre, giving a similar outline to the bag and known as a "waterfall". Drops also hung from the arms and canopies, contributing to an overall impression of almost overwhelming sumptuousness. Such a chandelier required hundreds of cut-glass pieces, and often well over 1,000. A Regency chandelier of any great size looked – and was – heavy: gone was the sense of glass forms dancing almost weightlessly in the air that characterized the neoclassical styles. The inner, supporting structure of the chandelier was completely hidden, disguised by the great swell of its outer form. The work involved in the making of such a creation was breathtaking – and so, inevitably, was the price it could command. A unexpected incidental advantage of the design was that it was later to prove highly sympathetic to electrification, since any number of bulbs could be concealed within the capacious tent and bag.

The United States had its own distant cousin of the Regency style, with tiers of hoops and prisms but few, if any, festoons of drops. A painting of 1822 by John Searle shows the interior of the Park Theater, New York, lit by just such a fitting.

The Regency period saw the creation of one of the most extraordinary collections of chandeliers ever made, which can still (after some adventures) be seen at the Royal Pavilion at Brighton on the south coast of England. Far from being typical of the Regency style, they accord with the shameless luxury and

Above: *This example in the Villa Lila, Cuba, by contrast to the chandelier in the left-hand picture, is solid, weighty, and clearly designed to impress.*

Left: *The cage form of this chandelier hanging in a Brussels apartment is festooned with large drops and other decorations to create an impression of airy grace.*

Above left: *Cool greys and neutrals accord well with the sophisticated lustre of a crystal chandelier in a bedroom in Marina Ripa di Mienas' Roman home.*

Above right: *This exquisitely delicate arrangement of graceful metal arms and languid festoons of crystal drops is a thing of beauty, with or without its candles.*

oriental exoticism of the interior decoration of this palace-by-the-sea, and as such are unique. To light the Banqueting Room, Parker's company created an elaborate gas-powered chandelier, or gasolier, installed in December 1821. From a hoop supported by chains sprout arms sporting glass shades in the form of lotus flowers, while below hang countless strings of shimmering round glass drops, some in the form of fringing, some in festoons, some gathered into tassels. The whole creation hangs from a silver dragon on the ceiling, set in a halo of painted lotus leaves. There can be few more bizarre gasoliers, and even fewer still hanging in the surroundings for which they were originally created.

Parker's company continued to be a leading maker of lead-crystal chandeliers throughout the nineteenth century, with competition from significant rivals such as Osler's of Birmingham (initially T. Osler, later F. & C. Osler). Following the repeal of a heavy duty on glass in 1845 the English glass trade burgeoned, and chandeliers frequently became gasoliers and even, towards

the end of the century, electroliers. Osler's supplied chandeliers to royal households both at home (including Osborne House, Queen Victoria's coastal retreat on the Isle of Wight, and Buckingham Palace) and abroad, making a particular market for itself on the Indian subcontinent. Indeed, India represented a market of unsurpassed wealth (far greater than the United States) throughout most of the nineteenth century.

The nineteenth century was a time of new and dramatic developments in the history of the crystal chandelier. Three principal factors together prompted this period of change. Firstly, industrialization and the growth of manufacturing wealth meant not only that there was more money in circulation, but also that those who had it (especially those to whom it was a novelty) were eager to show and enjoy their wealth by spending it. Secondly, chandelier design was quick to respond to the many new methods of producing light that was brighter, cleaner, or more convenient than candles, using a variety of power

Above: *This Paris apartment, designed by Nye Basham, displays another successful variation on the theme of neutral tones, uncluttered lines, and glorious antique crystal.*

Above: *This arrangement of an elegantly spare crystal chandelier in a minimalist white-and-stainless steel kitchen displays not only a sure eye for dramatic effect but also a refreshing touch of humour.*

Right: *Drops on a crystal chandelier bought in a French flea market.*

sources. These included colza oil, kerosene (its American name) or paraffin (British), and gas. Candles improved, too, becoming ever cheaper and cleaner, and continued in general use up to and after the dawn of the age of electricity in the 1880s. Thirdly, other regions such as France, the Baltic, and the USA now entered the picture in force.

What is thought to be the first glass chandelier ever made in America dates from 1804. In shape it is distantly related to the Regency style, with a metal hoop holding six short, upward-curving arms for lights. Below the hoop hangs a bag formed from strings of square-cut drops, finished at the bottom with a circle of icicles. Glass icicles also hang from the six candle nozzles, and from the small canopy or coronet at the very top of the chandelier, to which are attached the chains supporting the metal hoop. The hoop itself is charmingly decorated with small upstanding brass leaves or fronds. Though related to the Regency style, this chandelier nevertheless displays an approach that is all its own, perhaps because the designer, believed to be Peter William Eichbaum, was of German origin rather than British. Visually, the emphasis is laid on the bag and arms. There is no tent shape above: instead, the brass chains are relatively short and entirely visible. Now hanging in the Pennsylvania Room of the Carnegie Library in Pittsburgh, this piece is

known as the Lafayette Chandelier, a reference to the fact that it lit General Lafayette's visit to the Pittsburgh Mansion House in 1825.

This chandelier is thought to be the result of a collaboration between three men: General James O'Hara, glass manufacturer, enthusiast for the elegance of crystal chandeliers and driving force in the project; William Price, English-born brass founder; and Eichbaum himself, who at the time ran a hotel by the name of The Sign of the Indian Queen, though he had formerly worked in the glass industry. O'Hara's motivation in proposing the project was apparently his conviction that the Pittsburgh glassworks would gain positive publicity from the manufacture of chandeliers. The glass for this great chandelier was made at his own factory and cut by Eichbaum. Over the next few years, at least seven other chandeliers were to be made locally. The largest is believed to be the one presented by O'Hara to the First Presbyterian Church in Pittsburgh in 1804, which had twenty lights.

There is a striking difference, however, between this charming but modest chandelier and the sophisticated concoctions found hanging in the villas and mansions of wealthy families in Boston and Savannah a few decades later. By the middle of the century the American population had swollen, from around five million to twenty-three million, and so had the market for glass. No doubt some of the chandeliers made during this time (and before) had been imported from England and elsewhere, but only a very few, and certainly many fewer than the number of chandeliers in America that claim an English or Irish provenance.

Above left: *Two or more identical or similar chandeliers hung in a line along a room, or two chandeliers seen at opposite ends of a vista through several rooms, make an even greater impact than one hung alone.*

Above: *In contrast with the interior on the left, here a single chandelier makes a bold impact hung in a double-height space.*

Left: *Stone, paintwork, and fabrics in shades of white and cream provide a restrained setting for a relatively simple and discreet chandelier decorated with strings of crystal beads.*

In 1950, Dorothy Daniels spelt out the facts bluntly in her authoritative work, *American Cut and Engraved Glass 1771-1905*: "Probably one out of ten cut glass chandeliers hanging in American homes and now labelled Waterford ever saw Ireland". The same is true of cut glass in general: "The possibility of English origin is particularly remote…any piece of cut glass known to have been in this country before 1830 can be accepted as American until proved to be English or Irish", usually through family documentation. Many proven European pieces are now in museums.

One of the ways in which early American glass can be distinguished from imported varieties is by its clarity. Across the world, the mineral manganese dioxide was added to the basic silica when making glass, in order to counteract the effect of impurities. But American silica was purer than its counterparts and needed little manganese. Over time, glass containing manganese is liable to take on a bluish tinge or "tinct", whereas old American glass tends to remain clear. Another reason for this comparative clarity, especially from the nineteenth century onward, lay in the fact that the American industry was a young one, unhampered by either history or old machinery, and able to adopt the best new manufacturing methods. With glass, this meant gas-powered furnaces that produced rapid fusion of the raw materials (and likewise steam-driven power for cutting), slow fusion being another cause of discoloration with age.

Left: *A set of three dazzling chandeliers lights a spacious passageway in a Florentine palazzo.*

Far left: *A crystal chandelier made by the distinguished French glassmaking firm of Baccarat, founded in Lorraine in eastern France in 1765. Production of chandeliers began in 1824 and has continued ever since.*

Above: *The lovely chandelier in the Temple of the Winds, Mount Stewart, County Down. Built in 1780 to designs by James Stuart, the Temple of the Winds is one of the most outstanding garden buildings in Ireland, offering breathtaking views over the famous gardens (a World Heritage Site) and Strangford Lough. Mount Stewart is a National Trust property open to the public.*

Right: *An impressive chandelier draws the eye upwards, in this case to an imposing coffered and gilded ceiling painted with an array of faux marble effects.*

Some American glass houses, including notably the New England Glass Company, also coloured their glass for decorative effect, adding preparations of for example sulphur or chromium (to produce yellow) or gold or copper (for red).

The numerous companies making or selling a range of lighting fixtures and chandeliers in nineteenth-century America included Mitchell, Vance & Co., Cassidy and Son, J.B. Colt & Co., John Early & Co., H.G. McFaddin & Co., George Dummer & Co., and F.H. Lovell & Co., all of New York; R. Williamson & Co. of Chicago; the United States Glass Company of Pittsburgh, Pennsylvania; Hobbs, Brockunier & Co. of Wheeling, West Virginia (a prominent glassmaking centre); the Mount Washington Glass Company of New Bedford, and McKenney and Waterbury of Boston, both in Massachusetts. In their catalogue for 1893 the latter declared: "We light the world". Mitchell, Vance & Co, meanwhile, had their eye on the European competition when they made the following claim in their catalogue of 1871: "The glass chandeliers are equal, if not superior, to the celebrated Osler manufacture (English), which have been heretofore acknowledged the best in the world". By inference, this reflects the continuing enthusiasm at the top end of the market for chandeliers of European manufacture. In his *Sketches of America* (1818), the English traveller Henry Bradshaw Fearon noted that "At Page and Bakewell's glass warehouse I saw chandeliers and numerous articles of cut glass of a very splendid description...It is well to bear in mind that the demand for these articles of elegant luxury lies in the western states. The inhabitants of eastern America being still importers from the old country". Cut-glass manufacturers sought to emulate English and Irish production and then sell it across the country: "The glass of Pittsburgh and the points adjacent", wrote Samuel Jones in Pittsburgh in the year 1826, "is known and sold from Maine to New Orleans".

Chandeliers and other items of fine cut glass were sold through shops such as jewellers and retailers of household glass and china. An intriguing feature of the nineteenth-century glass trade in America, as described by letters in the extensive archive of T.G. Hawkes (now at the Corning Museum of Glass,

Above: *Cut drops in a variety of shapes and sizes. The process of cutting glass derived from the bevelled glass used in making mirrors, and soon spread to every possible facet of crystal chandeliers.*

Left: *Crystal chandeliers echo each other in magnificently baroque fashion in the dining room at the Château de Groussay, near Versailles.*

New York), founder of the Steuben Glass Company of New York, is that it was acceptable for a customer to bargain over the price of goods, at least in the 1880s when competition for customers was keen.

The Pittsburgh and Wheeling glass manufacturers were among the most prominent in nineteenth-century America. They were able to sell their glass chandeliers duty free, not only in New England but also further south, where there was less competition from indigenous glassworks. The precious cargo was packed with care into crates that were then shipped down the Ohio River to the Mississippi and onto eastern seaports. Thus the market expanded to include towns such as Charleston, Saint Louis, New Orleans, and Savannah, Georgia, where an eager clientele was waiting. Every one of the historic and museum houses now open to visitors in Savannah boasts a chandelier, some of them truly splendid. The Isaiah Davenport House on East State Street, for example, has extravagant chandeliers in both the dining room and the grand parlour. Construction of this Federal house began in 1818, the year when Davenport became an alderman, and it is thought that at least one of the chandeliers was a European import, made by Baccarat in France. The high quality of the building and its interior reflect not only Davenport's prosperity but also the personal interest that this former joiner took both in the overall structure and in the classical detail of the interior.

The greatest showcase for chandeliers in the United States was and remains the White House in Washington DC. In the years since President and Mrs Adams moved in as the first inhabitants, in November 1800, each successive administration has left its mark on the interior decoration. Sometimes this was because previous decorations were simply worn out by use, but often it was an expression of the enthusiasm of nineteenth-century presidents in particular for redecorating. This was never hampered by a protectionist attitude to the interior décor of the mansion, nor by any notion that the contents should be entirely American. A number of the fine chandeliers in the public and private rooms throughout the White House are traditionally labelled English, French, or Bohemian, though how many of these would pass muster with Dorothy Daniels is uncertain, and precise records of purchase and provenance are not always

available for nineteenth-century furnishings. There can be no confusion, however, about the redecoration of the East Room by Ulysses Grant (president 1869-77), which involved the installation of the massive tiered crystal chandeliers, in a recognizably Regency style, that had been commissioned for President Jackson's extensive alterations in the 1830s (at a cost of $9,000). Thriftily adapted for gas and with the addition of yet more glassware (shades for the flames), these now formed part of a highly ornate scheme that was lambasted as "steamboat Gothic". The East Room was renovated again in 1902, and during the Roosevelt administration (1933-45) the "steamboat" chandeliers were replaced by three large but more restrained Bohemian crystal electric chandeliers, more in keeping with the cool classical style introduced by the architects McKim, Mead, & White. The Grand Hall of the White House has three handsome chandeliers dating from around 1790 which are probably the work of William Parker.

The largest and most splendid chandeliers have almost always been created for massive buildings, be they presidential or royal palaces or public buildings such as opera houses. Indeed, no open interior space on a grand scale could be lit satisfactorily at the centre without the installation of a chandelier, since the light shed by wall sconces was simply too peripheral. Even the Spanish Riding School on the Hofburg in Vienna, created originally in 1735 by Josef Emanuel Fischer von Erlach, has splendid crystal chandeliers at its centre.

Few sights can have been more magical than the Hall of Mirrors at Versailles (created between 1678 and 1686) in its heyday, hung with three rows of magnificent lead crystal chandeliers, punctuated by torchère candelabra placed along its length, and with the light from thousands of candles reflected in the mirror glass lining the walls.

Versailles is of course endowed with many beautiful lead crystal chandeliers. An exceptionally pretty pair, each with two tiers of arms and strings of crystal drops falling from a flowered coronet, hangs in Queen Marie-Antoinette's bedchamber. Chandeliers for special events, such as a festival or celebration in the state apartments, were not infrequently hired for the occasion. This is a practice that was not confined either to Versailles or to

royalty. Crystal chandeliers were available for hire for special occasions – such a transaction is mentioned in the accounts of the Duke of Devonshire's Chatsworth House in Derbyshire – when they were simply slung on a pole and carried through the streets to their temporary location. This undignified treatment, together with the effects of heat and wax and regular cleaning and repair work, doubtless contributed to the demise of many a fine piece.

The type of chandelier that we associate with French work has a different profile from the classic English glass chandelier (and indeed from massive examples such as those at Versailles). It is more open, with its main structural support supplied not by a stem or chains but rather by a cage or frame with prettily curved members, often gilded and with drops or candles in the central space. Like its English cousin, it has pendants and chains of drops. Instead of being massed together, however, they are spaced further apart so that they can be seen individually. The effect is ornate without being elaborate, and extremely delicate.

By 1900, the ironwork on French chandeliers was superbly refined and attractive, and unsurpassed in quality and craftsmanship. The stem might have leaves and stalks curling off it along its full length, for instance, each supporting crystal drops, beads, and flowers. The fine metalwork is always visible, both in the cage design discussed earlier and in the wide variety of other forms adopted by crystal chandeliers in France. For all their bags and festoons of drops, glass arms, and full panoply of other elements familiar from the pre-eminent English chandelier, they nevertheless remain distinctively French, never crowded or heavy, and always alluring.

Perhaps the best known and longest established maker of the most distinguished chandeliers in France is the firm of Baccarat, which continues to thrive and innovate to this day. The origins of Baccarat can be traced to eighteenth-century Lorraine in eastern France, where the Bishop of Metz held jurisdiction over the châtellenie of Baccarat. Wanting to make the land productive, he struck on the idea of setting up a glassworks powered by wood, a plentiful local material that could be floated to the factory site on the River Meurthe. In 1764, he successfully petitioned Louis XV for permission, pointing

Above: *A glimpse of a pretty crystal chandelier at the Castillo de Bendinas on Mallorca.*

Left: *A crystal chandelier in the White Drawing Room at Arlington Court in Devon, now owned by the National Trust but formerly the home of Miss Rosalie Chichester, who filled it with her many collections, including model ships, pewter and horse-drawn carriages. This fourteen-branch chandelier is believed to be of Waterford manufacture, dating from around 1800.*

Above: *An elaborate chandelier hangs from an equally intricately worked ceiling – but a potentially indigestible combination is relieved by the serenity of the chandelier's composition.*

Right: *A gracious and expansive crystal chandelier hanging from a decorative stucco ceiling, both equally delicate in mood and style.*

out the economic loss incurred to France by imports of glassware from Bohemia and the fact that local woodcutters were without work. Letters patent founding the Baccarat glassworks were signed on 16 February 1765 and registered with the parliament of Metz. The factory did not at first make lead crystal, however, nor was it the first to make lead crystal in France. This honour fell to the St Louis company, also in the Vosges, which started production in 1781. Baccarat followed suit in 1816, and in 1824 began making chandeliers, a line of production that has continued ever since. Its latest design for a crystal chandelier for the twenty-first century, Mille Nuits by Mathias, has a sharp, elegant look, identifiably modern in appearance and with the practical advantages of having detachable arms, for easy cleaning, and halogen lights (the transformer is concealed in the central body of the chandelier).

In spite of many vicissitudes in its fortunes during the decades following the founding of the company – the consequences of forced sales, revolutions and war – the factory survived and still stands on this original site. A high point for Baccarat was the year 1823, when Louis XVIII publicly admired its wares at the Exposition Nationale in Paris, and it was sold to a partnership including Pierre-Antoine Godard-Desmarest, a stickler for quality. Then, as again now in the twenty-first century, quality was recognized by the enlightened few as one of the keys to manufacturing success. Among other measures introduced to the company's working practices, raw materials were now scrutinized with care, resulting in the importation from the United States of superb American silica, and potassium. Later, an American subsidiary was established to sell Baccarat crystal in north America.

Like other successful manufacturers of chandeliers in Europe, Baccarat also looked east to increase its sales. Among its customers it counted the Shah of Persia, the Khedive of Egypt, and the Sultan of Turkey (the tradition continues: in the 1980s a Japanese subsidiary was established). According to a story from the heyday of the British Raj, the Maharajah of Gwalior ordered a fifty-seven-light Baccarat chandelier for a new pavilion, a gift from the British. But once the splendid piece had been installed, the ceiling proved unworthy of it. Crashing to the floor, the chandelier was smashed to pieces. Undaunted,

the Maharajah ordered another chandelier, but not without first taking the precaution of testing the newly reinforced ceiling by ordering his heaviest elephant to be paraded on the roof above.

Members of the Russian aristocracy formed an important part of the Baccarat clientele during the second half of the nineteenth century. Indeed, one-third of the workforce, which numbered over 2,000 in all, were employed in manufacturing goods for this market. Chandeliers played a prominent part in schemes for sophisticated Russian interiors at this time, as in other Baltic countries. By 1800, Sweden had seven glass houses and made at least some of its own chandeliers.

Russian chandeliers in particular have a distinctive look, frequently also to be found in other chandeliers in grand and historic settings around the Baltic. Like those favoured by the French, they have an open appearance, derived from an ironwork structure that is generally fine and highly visible. Some have outlines reminiscent of the Regency style, but without the massed glass beads or drops; some have a square "hoop" rather than a round one, with two or more short arms for candles sprouting from each corner. Many have an appealing flourish at their very apex, in the form of a fountain of drops falling from short, curved metal brackets. One style has icicle drops falling from sturdy swags, formed from metal wire, which dip between the arms around its middle. Others take a "dish" form, the dish (or dishes, one above the other) being hung from chains, and the arms clustered around the rim, in a style that tends to be made exclusively in gilded brass or bronze.

The main difference between an antique glass chandelier and a modern example is likely to lie in the fact that the latter is wired for electricity. Hence one of the great ironies that emerges when we use a chandelier of any period or origin to light a room today. We take electric light for granted: in fact it has become one of the most exciting tools of contemporary decorating. But most of the chandeliers discussed in this book were originally created for use with candles, and now we are seeing both chandeliers and the rooms in which they hang in literally quite a different light. The effect of bright electric light, especially where many bulbs are close together as on a chandelier, can result

Left: *One of the breathtaking chandeliers in the collection at the royal palace of Hampton Court, Middlesex. Hung with rock crystal, it has silvered heads of lions and unicorns, the royal heraldic emblems, decorating its frame. It hangs in the Queen's Audience Chamber.*

Above: *A rare and fabulous chandelier with pale blue opalescent glass arms and amethyst glass drops, now in the collection of the Metropolitan Museum of Art in New York. Dating from around 1790, it is believed to have come from the home at 43 Wall Street of Thomas Cornell Pearsall (1768-1820), commission merchant, ship owner and noted art collector. It was acquired by the Metropolitan Museum in 1968.*

Above: *These Bohemian crystal chandeliers formed part of the 1902 refurbishment of the East Room of the White House, Washington DC, by architects McKim, Mead and White, under the guidance of Mrs Theodore Roosevelt. This is the room – substantially unaltered since 1902 – where the first US president in residence, John Adams, had his laundry hung to dry, where Union troops were billeted, and where presidents including Abraham Lincoln and John F. Kennedy have lain in state.*

Right: *Fine neoclassical chandeliers hanging in the Cross Hall of the Grand Entrance of the White House. A third and larger chandelier hangs beyond the pillars to the left. Of the two in this picture, Martin Mortimer has written in his scholarly survey* **The English Glass Chandelier** *(Antique Collectors Club 2000),* "*They have plain six-sided arms, Van Dyck-bordered pans and nozzles and ormolu bands on their central vases. They date from about 1790 and can be attributed to William Parker*".

in glare, which is the enemy of effective lighting. It can also have a flattening effect. Candlelight, by contrast, brings a decorative plaster ceiling or wall panelling to life. Mouldings are accentuated, shadows move with the flickering light. In *The Decoration of Houses* (published in 1897) American novelist Edith Wharton and her co-author Ogden Codman Jr went so far as to lament even the brightness of daylight in "old Italian saloons". "Modern travellers", she declared, "should remember that such apartments were meant to be seen by the soft light of wax candles in crystal chandeliers".

In wealthy homes across Europe and America, wax candles were lit for special events, which were probably the only occasions on which a chandelier was put to use. More modest homes had to make do with candles made from animal wax, cheaper but correspondingly less efficient. Even wax candles had drawbacks. They consumed oxygen and created heat – the more candles the greater the heat, so that it was not unknown for ladies to faint from the effects. Wax dropped onto the floor (and people) below, and chandeliers had to be serviced: wicks had to be trimmed and burned-out candles replaced. The latter chore was avoided during an evening's entertainment by calculating how long the event would last, and installing a size of candle that would burn for at least this length of time. If the event was expected to last only a few hours, a size of candle that would burn for twice this length of time might be selected. The half-burned candles would then be stored away until the occasion of another evening entertainment that required only a relatively short burst of candlelight.

In the long history of candlelight, one of the most impressive spectacles ever to take place was the coronation banquet of George III of England in 1727. Guests were seated in near-gloom, awaiting the start of proceedings, when suddenly some 1,800 candles, in chandeliers, candlesticks, and wall sconces, were lit almost instantaneously, so that the magnificent hall was filled with a glorious and unaccustomed light. A clever system had been devised for lighting the candles, whereby a fuse dipped in sulphur trailed from wick to wick. Not so amusing, apparently, were the still-hot pieces of burned fuse that floated down on to the wigs and sumptuous garments of the guests beneath.

Left: *The extraordinary chandeliers in the Music Room of the Royal Pavilion, Brighton, conceived as inverted parasols and executed in the Chinese-Indian pastiche oriental style so beloved of the Prince Regent and so derided by his contemporaries (in his defence he pointed out that at least it wasn't French in inspiration).*

Above: *Believed to have been designed by Robert Jones and Frederick Crace and made by Parker & Perry, the chandelier in the Banqueting Hall at the Royal Pavilion is an immense affair, some 10 metres (33ft) high, weighing nearly a ton, and extravagant in every way: with the other chandeliers in the room it cost a princely £5,613.*

131

Above: *Detail of a chandelier in a New York apartment designed by John Stefanidis.*

Right: *The shimmering cascade of crystal drops and icicles of this classic chandelier in the St James's Casino, London, is both impressive and romantic, summing up for many people the glamour of crystal chandeliers.*

The advent of alternatives to candlelight in the nineteenth century gave rise to a debate about the relative merits of each method. Gas was popular for its efficiency, but its aesthetic quality was criticized – it was simply too bright. American author Edgar Allen Poe thundered that gas was "totally inadmissible within doors. Its harsh and unsteady light offends. No one having both brains and eyes will use it". Candlelight, however, was considered far more flattering; in particular it was more forgiving to the complexions of ladies of a certain age. Most people will agree that candlelight still holds charms for us today, which is why chandeliers are still made and sold for use with candles, and some antique glass chandeliers are left in their original state rather than being wired for electricity.

Another constant in the history of chandeliers into the present day has been delight in the use of colour, for example the use of colour in Venetian chandeliers has certainly contributed to their joyful appearance. Some coloured cut-glass chandeliers were made in nineteenth-century Paris and London for export to India and Persia, where they were especially popular, and the United States, where they also displayed a penchant for such frolics. Companies including Page and Bakewell and the New England Glass Company were well known for making coloured glass, at first by grinding down clear glass, adding colouring oxides and remaking it. The Metropolitan Museum of Art in New York has in its collections several antique lighting fixtures incorporating coloured or opalescent (milky) glass. Most stunning of all of these is a chandelier of around 1790, with pale blue opalescent arms, clear glass stem and nozzle fittings, and strings and drops of amethyst glass. The full provenance of the chandelier is still not known, but it is believed to have come from the home at 43 Wall Street of Thomas Cornell Pearsall (1768-1820), a commission merchant ship owner, and a noted collector of fine and decorative art. It was acquired by the Metropolitan Museum in 1968. Less sensational but none the less very cheerful and decorative are modern chandeliers decorated with fruit, foliage, and flowers formed from pressed coloured glass, and "bag" chandeliers constructed from strings of coloured glass.

ENLIGHTENED ECCENTRICS

Chandeliers come in all shapes and sizes – some of them more

unusual than others. This chapter celebrates special chandeliers

that it is neither easy nor desirable to slot neatly into other

categories. These chandeliers are imaginative, entertaining,

or simply out of the ordinary, and in that sense they are eccentric.

Some were conceived as novelties, others make historic

references, and others again are individual creations by

imaginative designers or craftsmen.

Previous page left: *A witty contemporary chandelier made from recycled blue-glass mineral water bottles, an old bicycle wheel, and chromed chain bought from a DIY store. By artist Sophie Chandler, it is one of a series of similar chandeliers she has made, which includes DIY Chandelier (1995).*

Previous page right: *A hot-air balloon chandelier of the type that enjoyed a vogue in the early nineteenth century, in the wake of the first successful balloon flight by the Montgolfier brothers.*

Left: *This unusual chandelier is formed from antique glass lenses formed into a ball, from which short leafy arms emerge.*

Right: *A unique and picturesquely crooked chinoiserie chandelier, complete with Chinese-style lamp, in an equally remarkable interior.*

The chandelier form is generous: it accommodates a wide range of talents and ideas. There is no particular pattern to these enlightened eccentrics. The chandeliers described and illustrated in this chapter do not follow any clear route of historical development in the manner of, say, crystal chandeliers. The only unifying factor here is creativity. On closer examination, admittedly, many of the most charming pieces are revealed to be continental European creations of the nineteenth and twentieth centuries. Amusing, decorative chandeliers often prove to be of French or sometimes Italian provenance. Today they are popular the world over, a great many of them finding homes in the United States of America. But true oddities crop up in a wide range of times and places. Though some, such as crystal galleon chandeliers, were clearly intended as witty and amusing conversation pieces for sophisticated salons, others, for instance antler chandeliers, were made in all seriousness and intended to be appreciated in the same spirit.

In the western states of America in the early nineteenth century, everyday life for most people required a considerable degree of resourcefulness and inventiveness, using whatever raw materials lay to hand. While in Germany or Scotland antlers might have been viewed as a sporting trophy, here they provided useful raw material for a household lighting device.

Antler chandeliers were also a popular accoutrement for a full-blown antiquarian or Scottish baronial look, of the type for which numerous nineteenth-century collectors and newly rich landowners displayed a weakness. The hall at Bowsholme in Yorkshire was just such a room. Furnished by Thomas Lister Parker in the early nineteenth century, its walls were hung about with

Left: *Madeleine Boulesteix makes witty, inventive chandeliers using recycled domestic objects and glass: "I started making chandeliers", she explains, "after finding about forty faceted glass drops in a pile of rubbish. Initially I thought I couldn't make a chandelier with them because that would be too obvious, but I succumbed".*

Above: *Another Boulesteix creation. "I admire inventiveness", she explains. "My outlook was weaned in the punk era in which, like other folk cultures, a lot was done with very little, a big zip became a tie, an old kettle a handbag, and a bunch of safety pins a brooch."*

Next page left: *An armillary-inspired chandelier with playful glided sun or cupid's head and arrow, one of three chandeliers on these pages which use circular forms to provide a focus for the chandelier's structure. From the Christopher Wray collection, this example is called Astro Deluxe.*

swords and a hunting horn, coats of arms and armour, paintings and portraits, heads of deer with antlers attached, and, hanging from the beams, an antler chandelier that is still in position today. Massive oak furniture completed the scene and contributed to an atmosphere of masculinity and historical resonance.

Modern America, meanwhile, nurtures a number of companies devoted exclusively to producing chandeliers and furniture from deers' antlers. They (and all who make or sell antler chandeliers) are keen to stress that all the antlers used have been shed naturally, just as a snake sheds its old skin. No animals are hurt in the process, it is claimed.

Galleon chandeliers provide a suitably frivolous contrast to antlers, being among the most unapologetically and sparklingly decorative of eccentric chandeliers. Composed of glass drops, they are generally cleverly designed and made: skill and ingenuity are required to ensure that the asymmetrical form balances, so that the galleon hangs straight, without listing to port or starboard, or dipping at bow or stern. Such pieces are occasionally seen in the churches of seafaring communities in the south of France, where they may simply have been decorative embellishments. Galleons are not, after all, fishing boats.

By the early twentieth century, however, galleon chandeliers were being produced commercially by the Parisian company Bagués, who continued

making them until the middle of the century. The artist and designer Erté, famed for his costumes for Mata Hari and for his fashion drawings for the American magazine *Harper's Bazaar*, is reputed to have had one in his home. Other variations on the theme were made in Italy. They vary greatly in size and in sturdiness. Some are light and whimsical, others solid and sturdy, and others again incorporate coloured glass as well as clear. This type of chandelier enjoys considerable popularity, and when examples find their way into smart antique shops in Paris and New York they command high prices. Yet a huge range of chandeliers in a wide variety of styles can still be found with reasonable price tags in markets and brocante shops across France.

Bagués made chandeliers in a variety of playful, decorative forms. A favourite was the basket of flowers, looking not unlike a piece of Cartier jewellery from the 1920s. Others included a crystal fish and a birdcage, complete with bird. Nor was Bagués the only manufacturer of such curiosities – rather they were a prominent producer and market leader. Another notable designer was Cheuret, famous among other specialities for making chandeliers of oriental appearance. One Cheuret bronze chandelier of around 1925-30 incorporates three herons in flight, their wings carved out of alabaster.

Previous page centre:
The sphere in this case is a blue glass ball that glows when the chandelier candles are lit; the circlet of little glass stars likewise twinkles.

Previous page right:
On this unusual and delightful silver lighting fitment inspired by the Arts and Crafts or Art Nouveau movements of the early years of the twentieth century, the four bulbs are suspended from a metal ring alongside delicate trembling hearts.

Left: *A galleon chandelier, its hull and even its rigging formed from rows and strings of glass beads and drops. Eccentric and delightful, galleon chandeliers also require considerable skill in their design and manufacture in order to achieve perfect equilibrium.*

Above: *A playful chandelier designed by Philippe Starck for the leading contemporary lighting company Flos, using cut glass decanters arranged on glass shelves.*

Right: *Montgolfier chandeliers designed by Kevin McCloud, inspired by an antique hot-air balloon chandelier he found in Italy. The early nineteenth century saw a wave of enthusiasm for hot-air balloons, prompted by the first balloon flight by the Montgolfier brothers.*

Chandeliers that take the form of flowers, with each bloom formed from several glass pieces wired together, must be among the most charming of eccentric lighting devices, as undeniably feminine as antlers are essentially masculine. As with all the chandeliers featured in this chapter, their charm lies as much in their appearance by day, when they are illuminated by natural sunshine and daylight, as in their evening guise, when they are lit from within.

Flower chandeliers are not made exclusively from glass. One of the most extraordinary chandeliers in the world is made of porcelain. The Salottino di Porcellana is a small room created for Maria Amelia of Saxony, Queen of Naples, in the palace of Portici – south-east of Naples – in which the walls and ceiling were made entirely from the Capodimonte porcelain discovered and developed by Maria Amelia's husband, Charles Bourbon, King of Naples. The chandelier, too, is made of porcelain, with arms sprouting charming little pansy-like flowers in blue or yellow with pink centres, or green with yellow centres; pink, speckled, orchid-like blooms with yellow centres; pink buds nestling in green leaves; golden tendrils winding along and among the branches; and at the end of each arm, a curly, parrot tulip flower, with petals curling back to reveal the candle nozzle. Delightful as they are, the flowers are only one element in the decoration of this extraordinary chandelier. At the very bottom an exotic bird, possibly a species of stork, wrestles with a serpent. Its beak is open, revealing the pink inside, and its breast is white flushed with pink, with every feather here and on the underside of its flailing wings meticulously depicted. Above the point from which the chandelier arms spring, meanwhile, sits a Chinese boy, his arm wound round the stem, which is the trunk of an exotic palm tree. On his shoulder, just below the spreading green and yellow fronds of the palm, sits a little grinning grey monkey.

The chandelier has experienced three great adventures. The first was in 1759, when the 3,000 pieces of the Salottino were finally completed and assembled at Portici, only to be dismantled again almost immediately when Charles became king of Spain and the couple moved away. In 1866, the room returned to the factory at Capodimonte. In 1943, finally, it was smashed to pieces in a bombing raid: what visitors now see is a painstaking reconstruction.

In the twentieth century, some designers displayed a special lightness of touch and sense of humour that imbued their eccentric chandeliers with an irresistible warmth of spirit. A chandelier in the form of dolphins leaping and diving, a light bulb sprouting from each snout, may seem eccentric to the point of being kitsch, but it undoubtedly has the power to delight and amuse. Such chandeliers do not take themselves too seriously.

Among the most charmingly eccentric chandeliers are those designed to represent hot-air balloons. These fanciful delights were first made in the early nineteenth century, soon after the first ever successful flight in a hot-air balloon designed by the Montgolfier brothers, Joseph and Michel: travelling through the air for some 10 kilometers (6 miles) in 1783, it caused a popular sensation and was given huge publicity. Some hot-air-balloon chandeliers are French, and others Italian; some were made in the traditional chandelier materials of bronze or brass and crystal, others have as their centrepiece a glass or ormolu ball representing the balloon. An exceptional creation by Claude Gallé, maker of gilded ironwork items to both Louis XVI and Napoleon, was displayed at the Exposition des Produits de l'Industrie Française in 1819. Over 1m (3¼ft) tall, it consists of a tôle globe decorated with tiny gold stars and encircled by a gilded band, itself embellished with the signs of the zodiac, six gryphons' heads each bearing a candle nozzle, and short candle-bearing arms, all delicately ornate. From beneath each gryphon hangs a strut, also decorated, the six struts together carrying the "basket" of the balloon beneath.

A strikingly similar chandelier, acquired by the Swedish king Karl IV Johan in the first half of the nineteenth century, hangs in the Swedish Royal Collection, and yet another from the same period may be seen in the J. Paul Getty Museum at Malibu, California. Both of these are further embellished with festoons of glass drops. Contemporary manufacturers, such as McCloud Lighting in England, have re-created this delightful form of chandelier in metal with a variety of gilded and antique finishes.

While undeniably intriguing, a few eccentric chandeliers are more gruesome than charming, with a special place reserved for examples made from human bones. One such bizarre manifestation of interior decoration

Above: *A more urbane example of an antler chandelier usually associated with Highland shooting lodges, baronial halls, Alpine retreats, and the Wild West of America shows how a sensitive approach can reveal the intrinsic beauty and grace of the antlers. Todays manufacturers only use antlers that have been shed naturally.*

Left: *The rugged and masculine pioneer spirit of this log cabin interior is underlined by the chandelier made from antlers – a useful resource gleaned freely from the wild at a time when materials were scarce.*

may be seen in the underground ossuary at the Sedlec cemetery in the former Czechoslovakia. Founded in the early thirteenth century, by the end of the fifteenth it contained the bones of an estimated 40,000 dead. Toward the end of the nineteenth century, a sculptor by the name of Frantisec Rint conceived the idea of using the bones to create a decorative scheme, to include not only a chandelier but also the coat of arms of the noble Schwarzenberg family. At whose behest Rint created his fantasy remains a mystery.

The ossuary chandelier has four arms, each fringed with medium-length bones, probably (ironically) from arms. Supporting each arm of the chandelier is a chain of gaping jawbones, most with at least some teeth intact. The four candle nozzles are placed on skulls arranged facing outward, and other skulls decorate the stem, which itself consists of a mass of pelvic parts. There is a ghastly air of black comedy about the whole affair, as though it were some kind of terrible joke. It is not, but neither is it particularly ghoulish. The serried ranks of bones, especially the skulls arranged in orderly patterns along the architectural lines of the building, serve rather as a poignant memento mori.

Rosenborg Castle in Denmark is not only home to the earliest known Venetian chandelier, but also boasts an example of one of the most extraordinary coloured chandeliers ever made. Made by Lorenz Spengler in the early eighteenth century, it is carved entirely from amber. The arms curl out from an ornate, pillared central baluster in the style of brass chandeliers, festooned with amber drops cut into squares (hung like diamonds, from their corners) and pear shapes. Very few amber chandeliers were ever made, and their cost must have been astronomical. The most famous example of all is now lost, though its reputation lives on. In 1701, Emperor Leopold I received an extraordinary gift from Peter the Great of Russia: the Amber Gallery, a room made entirely from the precious substance, for his residence of Charlottenburg in Berlin. In 1755, Peter's daughter, the Empress Elizabeth, moved it to her country palace, Tsarskoye Selo, outside St Petersburg. Its whereabouts were last known in 1941 when it was dismantled to protect it from bombing; it has never been seen since.

Above: *A detail of the astonishing chandelier in the equally singular Salottino di Porcellana at Capodimonte, a small room with walls and ceiling of porcelain, commissioned by Charles Bourbon, King of Naples, for his bride. The Chinese images were inspired by designs on wallpapers ordered from Paris.*

Right: *This chandelier, made from human bones, hangs in the underground ossuary at the Sedlec cemetery in the former Czechoslovakia and was created by sculptor Frantisec Rint near the end of the nineteenth century. It serves as a poignant reminder that we all come to the same end eventually.*

MODERN
MASTERPIECES

With the coming of the modern age, chandeliers become the subject

of a debate: with so much lighting available, is the raison d'être for

the chandelier lost or is it possible to reinvent the form to suit

contemporary lifestyles? The development of the chandelier from 1900

provides an answer, demonstrating that although the function of the

chandelier has changed, it still has a place in the modern interior.

At the dawn of the twentieth century, the status of the chandelier had not changed greatly for a century or more. Certainly, gas and electricity were now available as brighter, cleaner, less laborious sources of power for lighting, but they were still used to power a central, hanging fitting, probably of brass and glass and holding numerous lights. This chandelier (or gasolier, or electrolier) still provided the main source of light in the room, supplemented by wall brackets and/or table lamps. The prevailing light level you could expect to find in a moderately prosperous home after sunset was much better than before, but still nowhere near the levels we take for granted today.

By the end of the century, the very existence of the chandelier as a decorative lighting device was called into question. Vast leaps in technology meant that the electronics of modern lighting, with all the possibilities offered by tungsten halogen, fluorescent bulbs, and fibre optics, were quite literally space-age by comparison. Aesthetically, too, light fittings were hugely varied in appearance, presenting design choices that were almost baffling in their scope. In practical terms, lighting had become so widely available and was so bright that a new problem arose – how to limit light effectively, so that we could see our computer, organizer, and television screens clearly while still enjoying sufficient ambient and task lighting around the home and workplace. Instead of gloom, the enemy of effective domestic lighting was now glare.

The story of the modern chandelier begins during the years of World War II. In the earlier part of the century, the prevalent styles of modern interior decoration were Art Nouveau, Art Deco, and Modernism. Few examples of light fittings conforming to these design idioms could be called chandeliers. Instead, they incorporated lanterns and pendant lights encased in shades made of glass, fabric, or metal, such as Charles Rennie Mackintosh's lights for the library of the

Previous page left: *The glass chandelier form brought into the twenty-first century by artist Deborah Thomas with her Shards of Glass chandelier.*

Previous page right: *An exquisitely delicate contemporary chandelier looks like something the fairies might have made, with its gossamer-fine wires looped and spiralled around two hoops attached to a central support.*

Above: *Squiggles in the air: the Flexeramus chandelier from Christopher Wray, with twenty-four halogen capsule lights on chrome arms.*

Left: *An iron and glass chandelier by Annet van Egmond hanging above a yellow glass vase by Borek Sipek in Jan Des Bouvrie's house in Naarden, Holland.*

Above left: *The Arrow Chandelier by Lindsay Bloxam, of Bloxam and De Matteis in London, commissioned in 1999 for a private house in London. The shades are made from hand-dyed silk laminated with a secret formula that gives it a parchment-like quality.*

Above right: *The bulbs held at the ends of the twisty wire arms that make up this spidery chandelier are shaded by small cups. The wires can be bent this way and that at whim.*

Glasgow School of Art (pre-1909) or Josef Hoffmann's for the entrance of the Purkersdorf Sanatorium in Austria (1904).

Though admittedly few, some fine examples of chandeliers in these styles do nevertheless exist, such as the rare and handsome example designed as part of an Art Deco interior in Florence, Italy (see p.169). Art Nouveau chandeliers, meanwhile, their fluid forms cast in brass with glass shades, were made by the Quezel Art Glass and Decorating Company of Brooklyn, New York, founded in 1901 by the ex-Tiffany decorator Martin Bach. One example from around 1910 has five arms, each with a tulip-shaped glass shade patterned with iridescent leaf shapes; the arms have little sprays of leaves standing proud of them, and small chains finished with little brass balls dangle provocatively from the very bottom of the piece. The effect is charming. The early twentieth-century American Mission Style also produced some handsome light fittings, including chandeliers with bold, squared-off forms, sometimes decorated with curled sheet brass elements.

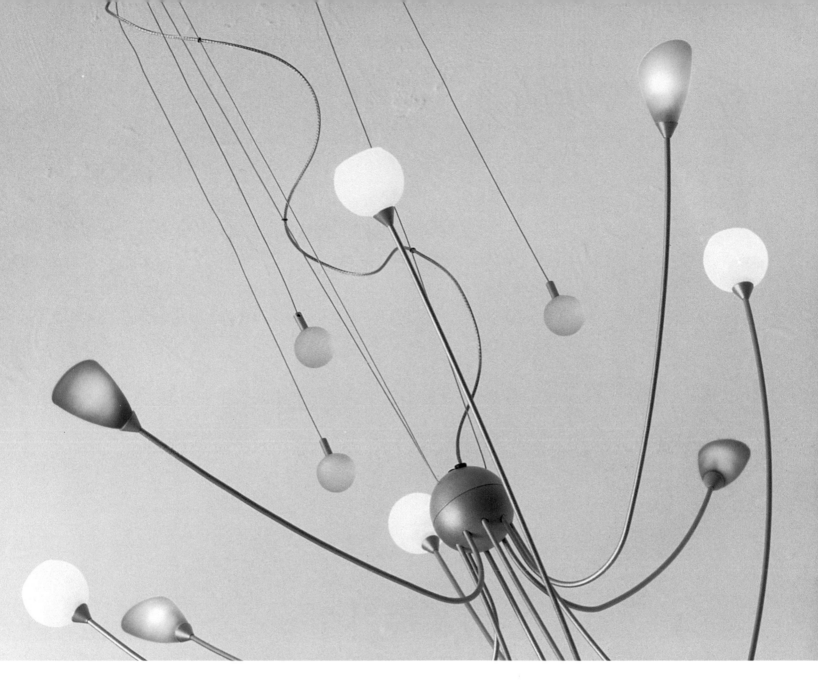

The nearest thing to a chandelier in a Modernist interior is perhaps a design of 1900 by the Austrian architect Adolf Loos (a great admirer of the technology of the light bulb), consisting of a metal ring with six electric light bulbs suspended from it at intervals, their wires threaded through the ring and extending up to a point on the ceiling, so forming a tent shape. References to both the early crown form of chandelier and the crystal-drop tent are clear, but at the same time the clean lines and lack of ornamentation are uncompromisingly modern.

Another rare "chandelier" from around this period is the multi-light fitting designed in 1920 by Dutch architect and furniture designer Gerrit Rietveld for the office of Dr Hartog in Maarssen in the Netherlands. This chandelier consists of a perpendicular arrangement of four short tube bulbs, two vertical and two horizontal, which is suspended by wires running through the stained oak endpieces of the tubes – the wires also supply electricity to the bulbs.

Above: *The Orbital chandelier, made by Lindsay Bloxam for the Picture House in Stratford-upon-Avon in 1998. The shades are made from PVC and the structure carries the low voltage system (twelve volts), so avoiding the need for separate wiring. A transformer is hidden in the ceiling.*

Right: *The Taraxacum 88S chandelier, designed in 1988 by Achille Castiglioni for Flos, the leading Italian lighting company. In the immediate post-war period, Castiglioni and other Italian designers embraced modern materials and aimed at something completely new in appearance, so providing inspiration for avant-garde lighting designers throughout the post-war decades.*

Left: *The surprising medium for this chandelier is porcelain. The work of ceramicist Jo Whiting, it consists of innumerable diminutive white porcelain tiles.*

Right: *A 1970 design by Ingo Maurer, a typographer and graphic designer who has become one of the giants of contemporary chandelier design, endlessly inventive and yet at the same time working identifiably within the chandelier tradition.*

Below right: *A chandelier designed by Peter Wylly of Babylon Design, London; another uncompromisingly contemporary design belonging to that breed of lighting fitment that is about focus and showmanship rather than the provision of a practical light source.*

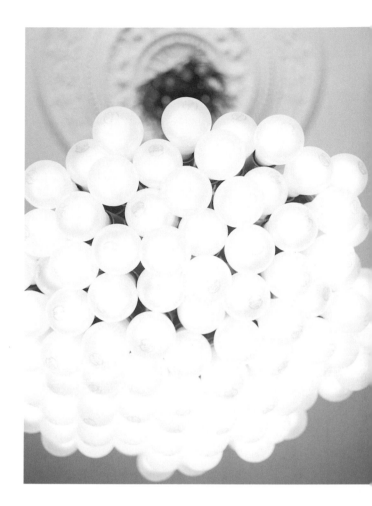

A similar design by Rietveld was produced by Het Goede Mcuble in the Netherlands in the early 1920s. By limiting himself in this case to three tubular bulbs, placed at right angles to each other – one vertical, one horizontal, and one projecting – Rietveld neatly defined the three dimensions, while also creating an arrangement that was more pleasing to the eye than the previous four-bulb version.

The two world wars changed popular attitudes in countless ways, many of them far removed from the political or military arenas. French fashion designer Christian Dior's New Look, unveiled in 1947, said it all. No fuss, no frills, (relatively) practical, and, above all, sexy and fun. War was over; this was a brave new world. As part of the war effort, industry and technology had benefited from huge injections of capital investment and brainpower. New materials and production methods emerged to greet designers whose vision of the world was radical, forward-looking, and modern. Plastics, for example, offered apparently infinite possibilities for completely new modes of expression in household furnishings, including lighting. In the forefront of this design revolution, illuminating the world with a veritable firework display of new and dynamic lighting designs, were the Italians.

Gino Sarfatti was born in Venice in 1912 and studied aeronautical engineering at the University of Genoa, but his fascination with and

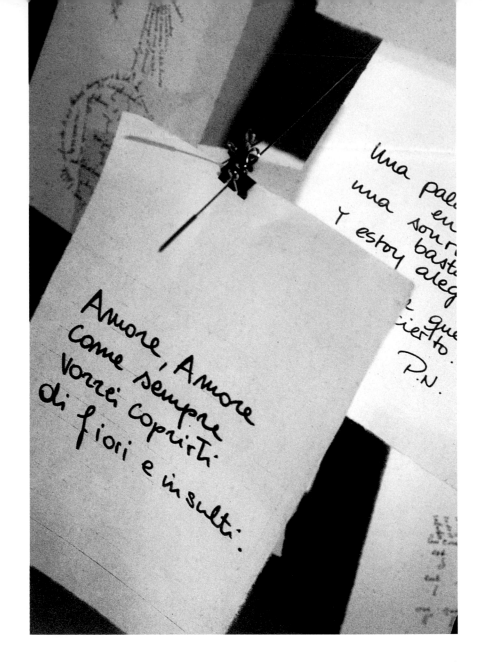

Right: *One of Ingo Maurer's Zettel'z series, Zettel'z 5 (1997), in which notes and poems are written on Japanese paper and attached to spokes of wire by small bulldog clips. Maurers' work has been exhibited at the Centre Pompidou in Paris and the Museum of Modern Art, New York, and he has collaborated with Issey Miyake, the Japanese textile and fashion designer.*

Far right: *The inscriptions on the Zettel'z series are all in black ink on white, in languages including Italian, German, and Japanese.*

understanding of engineering design and materials was quickly directed into more domestic channels. Just before the war, in 1939, he founded the lighting company Arteluce, based in Milan, and in the post-war decades he designed a huge number and range of lighting fittings using avant-garde forms and materials. Arteluce, according to Lesley Jackson in *The New Look: Design in the Fifties* (1992), "acted as a liberating force in the field of international lighting". The architect Alberto Rossi described Sarfatti's designs as having a "new energy", into which other lighting designers quickly tapped, flattering his originality with near copies.

One such design, created by Sarfatti in 1940, is a chandelier with tubular spokes of brass or chrome-plated copper, of different lengths, darting out from a central point, each with a bare bulb set into the end. It is undoubtedly a chandelier, yet it looks uncompromisingly modern and exudes a sense of celebration. Its festive air appealed to competitors – a chandelier made by the Stilnovo company in the late 1950s bears a striking resemblance to it. Sarfatti's chandelier 2097 (1953) has fifty bulbs, each sticking up from

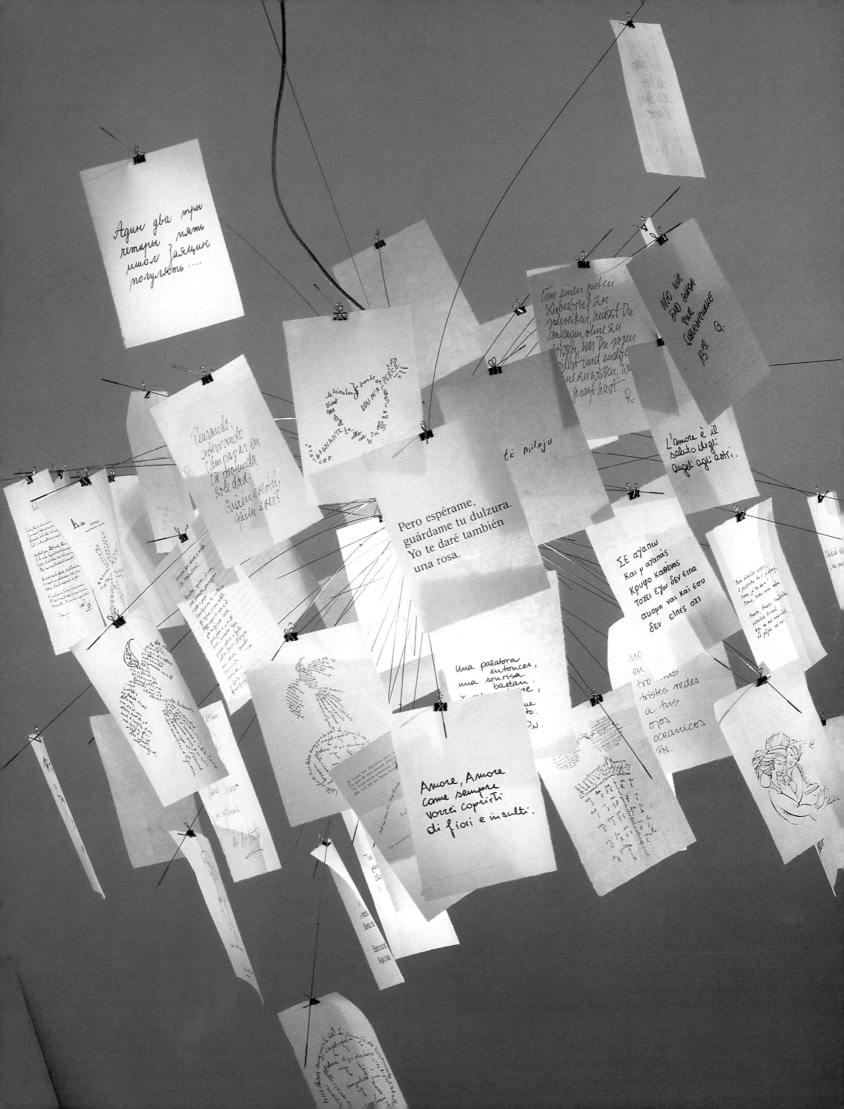

the end of a supporting metal arm and trailing its plastic flex in a loop back to the central stem of the fitting, a sturdy steel tube. The oval outline and tiered arms are strongly reminiscent of classic crystal chandeliers, yet the materials and styling are uncompromisingly modern.

Another Sarfatti lighting creation consisted of a collection of double-sided plastic discs, of different sizes and colours, hanging at varying heights from a framework of bent steel rods, which were attached to the ceiling. This colourful fitting echoed wonderfully the mobiles created by the twentieth-century American sculptor Alexander Calder. Sarfatti himself was happy with such references: he was not a designer who adhered slavishly to the principle of austere functionalism.

Sarfatti's broad range of references reflects the fact that Arteluce was much more than just a lighting company. At their premises in the Corso Matteotti in Milan, leading designers of the 1950s and 1960s met to thrash out the fundamental design questions of the era. In 1974, when he was in his sixties, Sarfatti sold the company to another Italian-based lighting enterprise, Flos. The company thrives to this day, and continues to manufacture and sell designs by Sarfatti (including the 2097 described above) and others of the period, which still look fresh and modern.

Other dynamic, contemporary Italian designers who stand out from their talented peers are the brothers Piergiacomo, Achille, and Livio Castiglioni, all three of whom trained as architects at the Milan Polytechnic. Piergiacomo and Achille's designs for furniture, a vacuum cleaner, seating, and other elements of interior design won them high acclaim from the outset, and some have become design icons – the Mezzadro stool, for example, formed from a tractor seat screwed to a support (designed in 1957 but not in production until 1971), and the Arco lamp, an elegant arc of steel sprouting from a marble base and culminating in a simple domed shade (first produced in 1962). In 1988, Achille Castiglioni designed the Taraxacum 88S, another chandelier still produced and sold by Flos which has inspired countless other designs. The principle was beautifully simple: bunch a number of bulbs together like a bouquet of flowers and suspend it from the ceiling. The form

Left: *Another chandelier by ceramicist Jo Whiting, this time a monumental piece commissioned for the Aurora restaurant at the Great Eastern Hotel in London. The countless porcelain tiles of the outer shade have a gauzy finish, created by a process discovered accidentally. Inside, uplighters illuminate the stucco ceiling and downlighters give directional light, while other lamps give life to the tiles.*

Above: *Stairwells are notoriously difficult to light: this fabulous contemporary solution tumbles like fresh cool water down the centre of a minimalist chrome spiral.*

and function of the chandelier are thus fulfilled with little more than the bare basics – light bulbs and wiring.

The refreshing modernity of chandeliers created independently by Gino Sarfatti and Achille Castiglioni provided inspiration to forward-looking lighting designers (such as Perry King and Santiago Miranda) through the arid decades of the 1970s and 1980s, when at worst chandeliers were firmly out of fashion, and at best they were generally seen as a retrogressive and historical element in the style anglais or country house look.

Alongside the frilly country cottage look, the other prominent style in the 1970s and 1980s was self-consciously modern, all mirrors and modular seating in shades of brown, green, and yellow or orange. Favoured forms of lighting consisted of wall-mounted spots with brown enamelled or brushed aluminium shades, or recessed eyeball ceiling spots. Happily, however, the lighting technology and pared-down approach of the 1990s was waiting patiently in the wings.

Left: *A collection of milk bottles with straws in a refrigerator? No: in fact this is Lights by Tejo Remy, an amusing take on the contemporary chandelier.*

Right: *The Fuscia chandelier, designed by Achille Castiglioni in 1996 for Flos lighting. This chandelier is available in a variety of configurations, including a single bulb and shade, three bulbs and shades, eight bulbs and shades arranged in a square, or twelve in a longer, narrower arrangement.*

Halogen lighting had first been used in domestic interiors in the early 1970s (though Achille and Piergiacomo Castiglioni had designed the Toio floor lamp, incorporating an industrial halogen lamp, as early as 1962). Twenty years later, halogen was established as the wonder light source of the future. Interior decoration shook off its fussy, frilly look and instead turned for inspiration to bare texture and colour, to touch and feel. The clean, bright light provided by ever-smaller tungsten halogen bulbs, controlled by advanced electronic transformers and dimmers, provided the perfect environment for contemporary living. Lighting once again took centre stage, but this time in an uncompromisingly modern guise.

The two giants of the world of contemporary lighting design at the very end of the twentieth and beginning of the twenty-first century are Dale Chihuly and Ingo Maurer. Each in his own way has adopted the traditional chandelier form and taken it forward in an idiom that is entirely modern. American Dale Chihuly is a glass artist, a master craftsman who has brought glass-blowing to

Above: *A delicate miniature chandelier by John Taylor and Anna Deacon of Delusions of Grandeur, made from fine wire and glass beads and designed to hold matchstick candles of the type used to decorate birthday cakes.*

Right: *A chandelier constructed from hoops and glass cups designed to hold nightlights, hanging in a Milanese home designed by architect Paola Navone.*

renewed prominence in projects around the world. The scale of his glass chandeliers is often thrilling, and the detail astonishing. Ingo Maurer is a German who trained as a typographer and graphic designer before turning to lighting as the medium in which he found self-expression. Both men's work has been acclaimed in exhibitions around the globe. Maurer has exhibited at the Centre Georges Pompidou in Paris and the Museum of Modern Art, New York, and has collaborated with the Japanese textile and fashion genius Issey Miyake; Chihuly at the Musée des Arts Décoratifs in Paris and the Powerhouse Museum in Sydney, amongst many others. Chihuly has also received countless scholarships and awards, and in 1992 was awarded the honour of National Living Treasure of the USA.

Ingo Maurer designs many different types of lighting, including floor, wall, table, and ceiling lights. His hanging ceiling lights can be considered chandeliers by virtue of the fact that their structure and light are fragmented, unlike a single, contained pendant fitting. The image of his most famous chandelier, Birds Birds Birds (1992), has been widely disseminated, probably because the piece manages to combine humour and charm without lapsing into sentimentality. On Birds Birds Birds, individual light bulbs each have

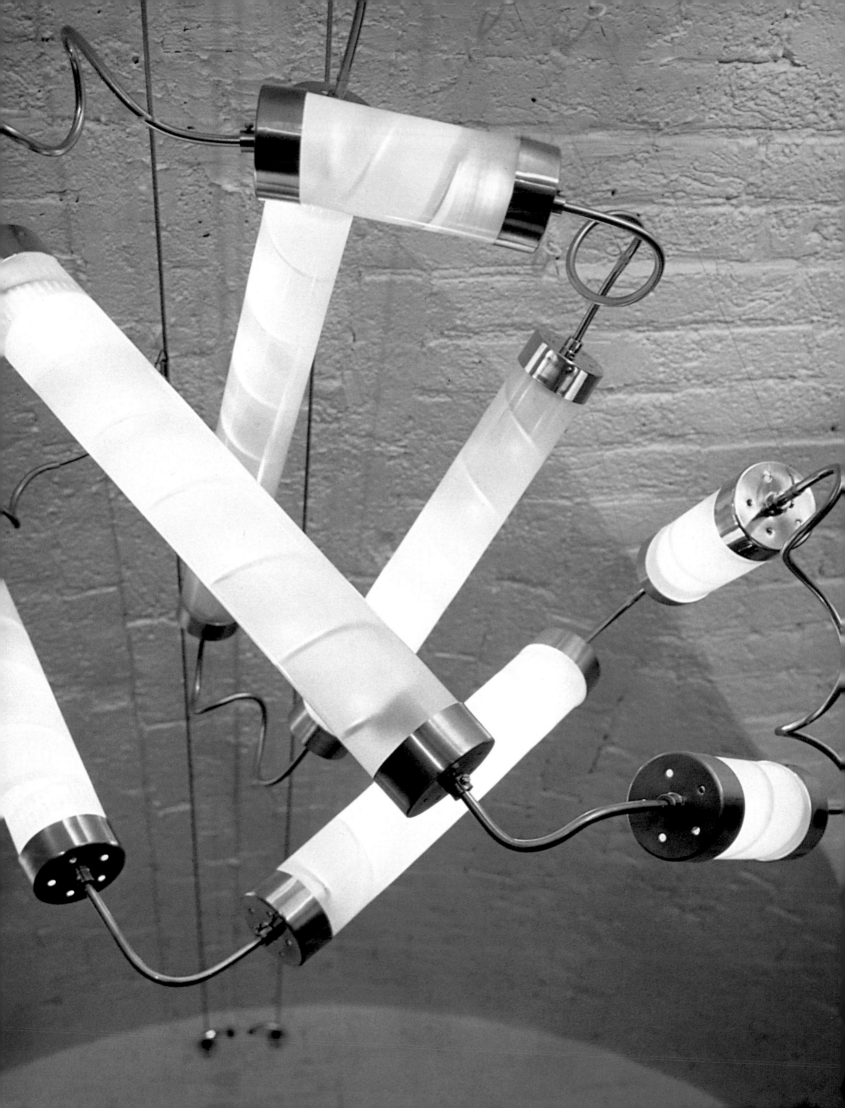

a pair of little wings made from goose feathers, and each bulb has its own supporting wires (one structural, one electrical) sprouting from a central metal rod. The bulbs do indeed look like creatures caught in animated flight, frozen for an instant. The chandelier provokes in the viewer a smile and a moment of pure delight.

Three other examples of Ingo Maurer's work display the designer's ability to break with the past while at the same time creating something that is identifiably in the chandelier tradition. One is the poignant Zettel'z series (1990s), in which a collection of rectangular pieces of Japanese paper is inscribed with drawings and messages, and each piece is held by a bulldog clip near the end of a wire arching out from the central light source. The pieces of paper are staggered, the overall profile of the chandelier being a broad rectangle or oval (depending on the exact model number), with fewer pieces around the periphery. The inscriptions are in many different styles of handwriting (including one musical manuscript), all in black ink on white, and in different languages including Japanese, Italian, and German. Porca Miseria! is constructed from pieces of (mostly) broken china that seem to explode from the central light source: a moment of arrested action like Birds Birds Birds. Fly Candle Fly! (1996) is another visual delight, a huge lit candle seemingly floating upright above the centre of the table. Maurer takes our expectations of what a lighting fitting should be and tosses them aside, surprising us with every-day elements from the world around us – white china, light bulbs, notes on scraps of paper – which he incorporates into his chandeliers. He transforms the usual into the unusual, with a lightness that is his touch of genius. His chandeliers are all astonishingly simple in appearance, though technically complex. Their scale is human where Chihuly's is monumental.

Dale Chihuly constructs huge chandeliers from hundreds of blown-glass pieces. The material itself is the source of his designs, and in this sense his chandeliers are a part of the long tradition of European and American glass. He was the first American to be allowed to work in the Venini glass factory on Murano, and it was in Venice that one of his most astonishing projects culminated in 1996. Called Chihuly Over Venice, this involved

Above: *The dining room of an Italian Art Deco apartment, complete with rare and handsome Art Deco chandelier with distinctively geometric lines.*

Left: *One of a collection of contemporary lighting fittings produced by the design partnership of lighting designer Lindsay Bloxam and Dr Cristina De Matteis, a scientist working in molecular design. Called the Mb Light, it represents the molecular structure of the protein molecule myoglobin. The design was funded by the National Endowment of Science, Technology and the Arts.*

Chihuly blowing glass with teams of local craftsmen in some of the most outstanding glass factories in the world, including Hackman at Nuutajärvi in Finland, Waterford Crystal in Ireland, and Vitrocrisa at Monterrey in Mexico. The pieces made at these glass foundries were then shipped to Venice, where they were assembled into fourteen huge chandeliers. These were then hung in selected locations around the city, including the Palazzo Ducale, the Giardino Sammartini, and the Rialto fish market. This is chandelier-making on a conceptual scale, rather than with an eye to the lighting of interior spaces. In Chihuly's work there may well be a relationship between the chandelier and the space in which it is set, but it is always on the chandelier's terms.

Dale Chihuly made his first chandelier in 1992, for an exhibition of his work at the Seattle Art Museum. It came about almost by accident, as Chihuly himself describes: "It was a big show, the entire second floor, and there was an area that wasn't working. At the last minute, I had the glassblowers start making a very simple shape that a beginning glassblower could almost make. I put ten or fifteen blowers on the project and we made the whole thing in a few days, in the ten-day period before the show opened."

This massing of countless glass shapes has become the hallmark of Chihuly's chandeliers. "It was yellow, and when we put it up it was twelve feet high and must have weighed 1,000 pounds. And it worked. A chandelier can play such a pivotal role in a room. It sort of anchors the space and allows the eye to expand around it." This conceptual approach to chandeliers, even to glass ones created by a man who has worked in the historic glass foundries of Venice,

Left: *The 2097 chandelier by Gino Sarfatti, a classic of modern lighting design, remains as thrilling today as when it was designed in 1958. Still in production, it is available from Flos. These examples may be seen at the Great Eastern Dining Room in London. One of the great figures of twentieth-century lighting design, Sarfatti, with his Milan-based lighting company Arteluce, has acted as a liberating force in the field of international lighting.*

Far left: *Ingo Maurer's highly influential Birds Birds Birds (1992) combines dry humour with beguiling charm. Each bare light bulb sports little wings made from goose feathers, a trailing electric wire and a wire that supports it in its upward flight.*

Above: *The work of Danish designer Verner Panton experienced a revival of interest in the last years of the twentieth century. His interiors use vibrant colours and focus on bold (often huge) lighting fixtures made from hundreds of separate elements.*

Right: *Chandelier with tassels by lighting designer Mark Brazier Jones, hanging in a London apartment.*

accords well with the new attitude required to carry the chandelier form into another millennium. No longer just a lighting fitting, it is a sculpture, a statement, an idea.

With their many pieces, Chihuly chandeliers also have an organic quality, as if they had grown over centuries like stalactites, or were a primitive form of life, like an amoeba or a sea anemone. Barbara B. Buchhols described them in the *Chicago Tribune* as resembling "underwater sea creatures with giant twisted tentacles…in eyepopping iridescent colours". In the same newspaper, Mary Daniels likened them to "flowers from the heart of a volcano". Many commentators find Chihuly's work alarmingly sexual. The glass globules on one have been described as being like glowing breasts, while another was dubbed as "nearly carnivorous in its sexuality" by an admiring critic, who also drew attention to Chihuly's "acute sense of colour and volume". The artist himself has said: "What makes the chandeliers work for me is the massing of color. If you take hundreds of blown pieces of one colour, put them together, and then shoot light through them, now that's going to be something to look at". He has a fascination with the way that a massive chandelier seems "mysterious, defying gravity".

Chihuly and Maurer are international giants, but there are countless other creative and original minds across the world who are fascinated by the chandelier form, and who design examples that delight as well as light. Dutch sculptor and designer Maroeska Metz is one. Her curly metal chandelier in her Amsterdam loft is a delight to the eye, and a reflection of the curls to be found on the chairs, tables, mirrors, and crockery that are also her own designs. Harry Allen, meanwhile, has designed his Plato range of floor, wall, and ceiling lights for George Kovacs Lighting in the USA. His Plato chandelier is space-age in appearance, but uses plates of glass, plain or coloured, to project delightfully quirky patterns on the ceiling and walls. The British designers Roger Parsons and David Hicks have each in their own distinctive way pursued the idea of bringing nature indoors, taking twigs and branches and incorporating these natural forms into chandeliers – a charming concept anyone with access to the countryside can reproduce (taking care not to be destructive: fallen wood or

garden prunings are best). New Yorker Marta Baumiller makes humorous chandeliers from hats. Back in Britain, Sharon Marsden frays nylon fabric and weaves fibre optics into this to make magical, ethereal forms that seem so light they might blow away in a draught. Even if there were no other evidence, the creations of such designers would be sufficient to convince you that the chandelier form is very far from dead.

British designer Tom Dixon's Jack light (1996) became an icon of the 1990s – a chunky light you could use on the floor or on a table, or even stack up one on top of the other to make a tower. He has also turned his talents to chandelier design, once again combining both humour and practicality. His Lightweight 2 chandelier (1995) for leading contemporary lighting company Foscarini makes witty reference to the traditional form with tiers of arms, and glances too at the art of Paul Klee, who liked to take a line "for a walk" in his drawings and paintings. It has three tiers, each with eight lights. Formed from lacquered metal, its fine tubular lines are curves on the bottom and top layers, and zigzags on the middle layer. Between the tiers are balls with protruding spikes.

Another designer working with wiry forms is Celestino Valenti. An artist and printmaker by training, born in Britain of Italian parents, Valenti currently draws in the air with galvanized wire, securing the joins with more wire ties or simply with twists. The only solder he requires is for securing the candleholders on to the arms of his chandeliers. These are fantasies in the air, frenzies of twirls and loops, criss-crosses, and concentric circles. His inspiration comes from anatomical drawings and the ornate costumes worn by the subjects of Elizabethan portraits.

Jo Whiting is another artist – this time a ceramicist – who has been drawn to the chandelier form. For the historic British china manufacturer Wedgwood she has created a porcelain chandelier consisting of tall, narrow tiers of china hanging in rings, creating a virtual column of pale light glowing through the translucent pieces. Another recent commission, in 1999, required eight chandeliers in two different sizes for the Aurora restaurant in London. At a glance, these look like giant pendant shades, but closer inspection reveals

Above: Orange Hornet Chandelier by Dale Chihuly, along with Ingo Maurer one of the dominating figures in contemporary chandelier design. Chihuly is a glass artist who fell almost by accident into making chandeliers at his 1992 show at the Seattle Art Museum, and who was to become the first American to work in the Venini glass factory on Murano. The Orange Hornet was made in 1993 and hangs in Portland, Oregon.

Right: A soft and delicate reinterpretation of the chandelier form by lighting designer Sharon Marston, who trained in mixed media and worked in costume design before starting to experiment with lighting. Her designs explore the sensual texture of her chosen materials – banana and pineapple fabric, nylon, tarlatan cotton, fibre optic threads, smooth Perspex and polypropylene – which she adapts by crimping, stapling and fraying.

Above: *Red Chandelier with Cobalt Blue Stem by Dale Chihuly (1994), once hung above the dining table of Charles Cowles in his New York apartment. Of the blue pistil-like form curling out of it, Cowles observed that his dinner guests were intrigued by the erotically surreal appendage.*

Above right: *Another very different light by Sharon Marston, made from lengths of perspex rod and called the Sticklebrick. Conceived as a wall light, it can equally well be placed on the ceiling in the manner of a chandelier.*

Far right: *Dale Chihuly's statuesque Cobalt Blue Neon Chandelier (1995, New York), one of the earliest examples of his use of neon as the lighting source in the centre of a chandelier.*

their technological complexity. The outer "shade" is constructed from hundreds of porcelain tiles, each only 5mm (⅛in) thick. Their surface is gauzy – a finish discovered accidentally by Whiting when muslin used to prevent the tiles sticking to the mangle left a ghostly imprint. Inside are three types of lamp: uplighters to illuminate the plasterwork ceiling in the restaurant, downlighters to give a practical, directional light, and lamps to give life to the tiles that make up the body of the chandelier. In this case, unusually today, the chandeliers actually provide the room's main light source.

Responsible use of the earth's resources and the recycling of man-made materials are themes that run through every aspect of interior decoration today. Some designers, such as Madeleine Boulesteix, follow these themes right through all of their work. Based in London, she creates witty chandeliers from "found" objects, usually household tableware and kitchen tools, occasionally incorporating crystal drops from old chandeliers. But there is more to her creations than a simple desire to be eco-friendly, as she explains: "I find trifle moulds and crinkly pastry cutters really humorous implements. Who decided they should be crinkly?" she asks. "And toast racks are perhaps the most absurd. What better way to cool down your toast too quickly than sit it in a rack so it is no longer able to melt the butter? I've never used a toast rack for toast or a pastry cutter for pastry, but they seem nice, jaunty objects with more potential, so I liberate them from their domestic duties by incorporating them in my chandeliers."

Chandeliers are no longer to be found exclusively in the drawing rooms and dining rooms of grand private homes, or in large public spaces such as ballrooms and hotel foyers. We buy them to hang in kitchens, bathrooms,

Above: *The sinuous, writhing chandelier created by Dale Chihuly for the entrance rotunda of the Victoria & Albert Museum in London. It took three days to install, building it up section by section. The chandelier has 755 pieces and weighs 1,041kg (2,337lb), of which 204kg (450lb) (represent the chain, armature and cable.*

Above: *Emerald
Chandelier (1997) by Dale
Chihuly. The experimental,
gourd-like forms of this
chandelier were made
in a lampshade factory,
the glass being blown
into lampshade moulds.
It hangs in Vianne, France.*

Left: *Detail of the Dale
Chihuly chandelier
in the Victoria & Albert
Museum, London, shows
the complexity of the forms
from which it is made.*

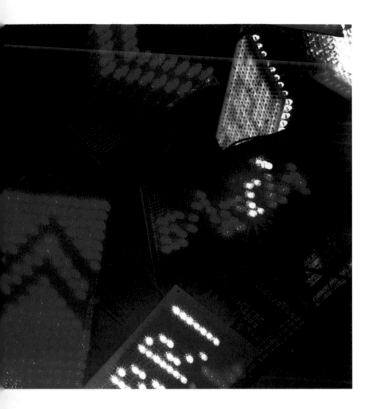

Top left: *Another in Ingo Maurer's Zettel'z series of chandeliers, this time using small panels resembling illuminated advertising hoardings, shown in its nocturnal manifestation.*

Below left: *The daytime appearance of the same piece.*

Right: *Porca Miseria!, an explosive moment frozen by Ingo Maurer. China appears to fly in all directions except that it doesn't. Witty and irreverent, this piece takes contemporary reinterpretations of the chandelier form a step further.*

bedrooms, and even outdoors. One of the most astonishing outdoor chandeliers is the Hurricane Chandelier created in 1989 by Unilight and designers Day Lipford and Associates for the Sandcastle Theater, Guam, the remote American protectorate in the Mariana Islands, between Japan, New Guinea and the Philippines. Their brief was to design and make a chandelier capable of withstanding the extreme weather conditions, including typhoons and hurricanes, that batter this part of the world. Their solution is a tall form with slim, galvanized steel arms and no flat surfaces to catch the wind. The result is a triumph, its soft, spidery profile a delight to the eye. It is also a practical success – as demonstrated three days after installation when it withstood a battering from Typhoon Ross.

The chandelier form will always be with us. We no longer need it for the purely practical provision of light – in fact in this respect it is indeed all but redundant. Instead, we need chandeliers to provide excitement in an interior, to give a focus. Artists are drawn to the chandelier as a disciplined form in which to express their talents. Customers and designers alike clamour for the unique qualities the chandelier brings to a space.

Award-winning architect Piers Gough has a theory regarding the continued success of the chandelier: "It lifts our spirits. The joy of the chandelier is the controlled explosion – the way its many parts cause light to refract and multiply in a cacophony of illumination – producing the same thrill as the sound of an orchestra in music. It doesn't increase the available light any more, but it does magnify its energising effect. Even in the twenty-first century, the chandelier is still a brilliant notion."

DECORATING
WITH CHANDELIERS

The choice of styles, colours, finishes, shapes, and sizes of chandelier available to us has never been greater. Indeed it can seem somewhat overwhelming. On the other hand, this means that for every scheme of interior decoration there is also, almost certainly, the perfect chandelier. This section takes a look at some of the issues and ideas relating to decorating with chandeliers, such as scale, style, and ways of presenting your chandelier so as to create different moods.

Massive wrought- and pierced-iron chandeliers, medieval in inspiration, are once again being produced. If you have a great hall, or other magnificently sized space, you will know that it demands lighting on a very grand scale. But be warned: a two-tier chandelier with a total of twenty-four lights is quite likely to have a diameter of 1.8m (6ft), be 3m (10ft) tall and weigh 500kg (1,100lb). Great care, therefore, should be taken, and professional advice sought, before considering the installation of such a mighty beast.

On a smaller scale, simple iron hanging candleholders are suitable for a look that might be described as neo-rustic. This is a wholesome, seemingly effortless shabby-chic style that revels in distressed paintwork and faded cotton fabrics. Neo-rusticism need not be out of place in a town or city, however. Here its bare-bones honesty is as in keeping with converted industrial buildings and pared-down contemporaneity as it is in an old country cottage setting. Many manufacturers offer a wide choice of finishes on their metal chandeliers. A polished finish (with or without beeswax) and plain matt black paint have now been joined by gold, ivory, and verdigris as standard finished surfaces, along with coloured undercoats in blue or red designed to show through a distressed surface. Some iron chandeliers are deliberately rusty, their dusty orange patina lending them an instant aura of age and history.

The great advantage of portable, candle-powered chandeliers is that you can hang them anywhere, provided that your ceilings are not too high. For example, an old low beam studded with ancient nails is the perfect host for an iron chandelier of any type, but you can just as well suspend it from a nail in the garden and light it on a windless summer evening (but check that the finish is suitable if you intend to leave it outdoors permanently).

Left: *Introduce an airy, springtime feel to an interior with pale colours, plenty of fresh flowers, and pretty glass chandeliers.*

Above: *Cascades of glass beads not only capture the light but also add an indisputable note of romance and glamour to any interior.*

A plain, sturdy form for a hanging iron candleholder is the ring. Medieval in inspiration, it consists of a flat hoop of iron (sometimes two hoops, one inside the other, attached by straight cross-pieces) with prickets (spikes for securing candles) standing upright at intervals. This might be hung from a single chain attached to the central junction of the cross-pieces, or (easier to balance and with less chance of spills) by three or more chains attached at evenly spaced intervals around the edge.

Simple modern chandeliers made of plain iron or twisted wire invite additional decoration for festive occasions in a way that more flamboyant, elaborate chandeliers perhaps do not. In winter, twist trails of ivy through the branches and round the stem, or dangle frosted pine cones from the arms at different heights. In summer, drape the arms with coloured ribbons or paper streamers, string coloured glass beads on to wire arms and curlicues, or festoon the whole chandelier with seasonal leaves and flowers. As always, use extreme care with flammable materials and never leave burning candles unattended.

Chandeliers similar to those created by pioneering Americans are an attractive choice and are still made in a wide variety of lively forms by lighting companies in the United States, whose catalogues you can browse at liesure on the internet. Typically, a pioneering chandelier might have a central wooden turned baluster to give weight and balance, with curved wire arms attached. If you are searching for a chandelier that is sympathetic to

Left: *A classic crystal chandelier is reflected, fragmented and multiplied by a random arrangment of mirrors in an otherwise coolly traditional setting.*

Far left: *A contemporary chandelier works well in an uncluttered modern interior in neutral tones, providing a discreetly witty focal point without being too dominant.*

existing furniture in your home, look around you at the shapes of your turned table legs and staircase banisters. Manufacturers of reproduction chandeliers are often willing to undertake special commissions, or you could find an old baluster at a salvage yard and commission a blacksmith to make and attach candle-bearing arms.

Whereas once no one below the rank of duke owned a silver chandelier, such an extravagance – or at least a silvered chandelier – now lies within the means of so many more people. Lighting fixtures finished with silver paint, silver plate, silver leaf, or even nickel and chrome are readily available from many outlets in a huge variety of styles. Their white-tinged finishes and the clean colour they reflect are popular in homes decorated in a cool, understated contemporary style.

Golden chandeliers, meanwhile, are still a hugely popular choice. A golden finish is achieved by manufacturers either by the traditional method of gold-leafing – still costly but incomparably effective – or by spraying gold paint, either by hand or mechanically, onto a brass, iron, bronze, or resin form. Some gold paints even contain a modicum of true gold to give it a more realistic effect. The forms taken by golden chandeliers today have no limits other than the manufacturers' ingenuity, from the traditional, with arms sprouting from a central baluster, to novel creations such as trumpets, crowns, and hot-air balloons. Whatever the form, a golden chandelier speaks of opulence, if not downright ostentation. It will be at home in an interior decked with fringing

and festoons, softened by luxurious fabrics such as velvet and gleaming damask, and surrounded by warm rich colours such as yellows and flame tones or by singing emerald greens and sea blues.

The familiar Dutch form of chandelier, with a brass ball and arms that curve away from it, has probably never been out of production in over five centuries. This form is recognizable to most from so many Dutch paintings, such as Emanuel de Witte's famous *Interior with a Woman at a Clavichord* (c.1665), which depicts an interior with fine fabrics and a valuable Persian carpet on the floor, but otherwise pared-down and uncluttered. Many paintings of Dutch interiors show bare wooden floors (albeit with good quality, fine wide planks) and walls bearing few (though often large and handsome) pictures or a single mirror. This mood is exactly in keeping with the direction that contemporary decorating has taken at the beginning of the twenty-first century. The emphasis has returned to texture and colour, on the natural or enhanced tones of the materials from which buildings, furniture, and furnishings are constructed. Although silver-toned metal finishes, such as stainless steel and chrome, have become hugely popular, brass has remained a much warmer and more approachable material.

There is no surer, quicker route to opulent decorating, on the other hand, than to install a crystal chandelier. Its mass of sparkling drops shimmering in the light of many candles or bulbs is enticing, exciting, romantic, and above all glamorous. This effect is enhanced if you paint the room a rich, glowing colour, perhaps a strong, velvety red, green, or blue. Hang framed mirrors around the walls to reflect the chandelier, and light candles along the length of the table or on side tables around the room, or both (always bearing in mind safety considerations). Another effect entirely can be created by giving your crystal chandelier a summery setting. Surround it with pale, floaty colours, such as candy pink or mauve, sky blue or sunshine yellow, with plenty of white and pale wood, and you will create an atmosphere of airy lightness. Match this with masses of scented fresh flowers and foliage and surround it with mirrors to make the very most of the available natural light.

A traditional Venetian glass chandelier will bring flowers of a different kind – glowing confections in glass – into your home. The famous name of Murano is so closely identified with high-quality hand-made Venetian glass that manufacturers in other parts of the world routinely counterfeit its production. The only way to be sure that you are acquiring the genuine

Right: *In a daringly dramatic and individual décor, a chandelier of similarly classic style serves as a useful and unexpected counterpoint to what otherwise threatens to be an overwhelming expanse of faux animal print.*

Left: *A flamboyant crystal chandelier's looks at home in this rich, sumptuous setting of jewel-like reds and golds, conveying a message of opulence and solid traditional values.*

Venetian article is to buy from a reputable source, such as direct from manufacturers on Murano over the internet. Alternatively, ensuring the authentic provenance of your purchase might offer the perfect excuse for a trip to that most bewitching of cities.

Don't be afraid of hanging quite a large chandelier – the visual impact will be all the greater. You want to avoid any physical impact, of course, so the bottom of the chandelier should hang several inches above the head of a tall person. The general recommendation is 2m (78in) from the floor – otherwise you run the risk of incidents such as the one described by Jean de la Bruyère in his *Caractères* (1688), in which a low-hung chandelier snagged and snatched off the wig of an unfortunate gentleman passing beneath.

Formerly, the cost of cut-glass chandeliers put them out of the reach of any but the very wealthy, and then usually only for a reception room where they would be seen by the widest possible public. Now, however, chandeliers of all sorts are available to suit a much broader range of budgets. Those grand reception rooms had high ceilings, whereas today's homes are more modest in scale and have lower ceilings. Manufacturers have taken this into account, however, and offer cleverly designed crystal chandeliers that require only a matter of inches, rather than feet, in which to hang or be fixed. After all, there is nothing quite like a crystal chandelier, or the nearest thing to it, especially in a grand or important setting.

CARING FOR YOUR FITTING

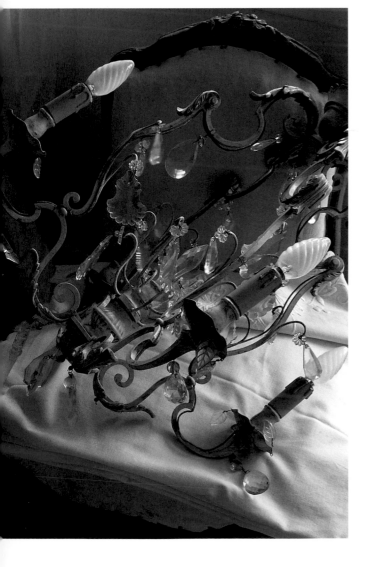

Once you have installed a chandelier in your home, the next (vexing) question is how best to clean it. This applies particularly to delicate and fragile glass and crystal chandeliers, as when dust settles on these it covers them with a grey film that not only dulls their colour but also reduces their clarity and glorious sparkle. Take advice from the experts, who have strong views on how to – and how not to – clean a crystal chandelier in order to restore it to its original shimmering glory.

When you hang a delightful concoction of sparkling glass or crystal pieces from the centre of your ceiling, you delight in the effect of glamour and sophistication that the chandelier immediately brings to the room. Probably the last thought in your mind is the question of cleaning it once the inevitable film of dust has quietly settled on it. And how much greater the concern when the chandelier in question is a huge piece, with thousands and thousands of glittering parts, hanging in the stairwell of a mansion or in an historic building or castle! Here the matter is further complicated by the question of access, of how to reach the chandelier, but in other respects the issue remains the same, whatever the size and location.

Experts who clean the finest chandeliers in the world – for monarchs, presidents, and prime ministers – are united and adamant on one point: spraying chandeliers, although it may seem the simplest method, is not the best way to clean them. The spraying theory involves using the right combination of chemicals, you simply spray the chandelier from the top down; the liquid picks up the dust and carries it down with it, dripping into a container or suitable absorbent material (such as dustsheets or old newspapers) laid beneath. In practice, say the experts, fluid gathers in every cup and indentation, so all of these parts end up having to be laboriously wiped by hand anyway. Alternatively, the solution leaves a stain where it has collected and eventually evaporates. There is also the danger of these chemicals seeping into the holes where brass pins hold together drops and ornaments. Corrosion of these vital metal parts almost certainly follows. There may also be a residue left on the surface of the glass after drying. It has even been known for strong spray-cleaning chemicals to strip the lacquer from the brass or bronze frame of

Left: *Bargains and lucky finds are still to be had on market stalls and in junk shops: a thorough, gentle clean will work wonders, and lost or damaged parts can generally be replaced.*

Above: *Specialist suppliers such as the London firm of Wilkinson, established in 1920, carry an extensive stock of antique crystal and glass pieces with which to repair or restore damaged chandeliers or market finds.*

a chandelier, which consequently oxidizes and blackens. This may also pose a potential danger to wiring. And this is all in addition to the obvious environmental implications of using chemicals unnecessarily (not to mention the unpleasant smell they may leave in your home).

Horror stories abound, reinforcing the message that there is no short cut to cleaning a glass chandelier. "There is only one way", says a leading expert, "which is to dismantle the pieces, clean them by hand and reassemble them". This does not mean, however, that the task is a difficult one to be dreaded or feared, but simply that it is not one to be hurried.

To make cleaning easier, when you commission an electrician to install your chandelier, specify a sliding ceiling hook that enables you to detach the chandelier from the power. This way, the entire fixture, including the stem, can be brought down for cleaning. Alternatively, and if your chandelier weighs more than about 15kg (33lb), have a small connector block inserted into the wiring at the top of the chandelier. To detach the fitting, switch off the power and unscrew the connector block with an electrical testing screwdriver containing a working fuse.

Throughout history, access to chandeliers for maintenance has always been a taxing consideration – and much more so when all chandeliers were candle-powered and the candles had to be serviced and changed on an almost daily basis. In previous centuries, the solution was to lower the chandelier by means of pulleys and ropes, with a counterbalance to provide stability and prevent the great weight of the fixture from crashing to the floor. The ring on the very bottom of many early brass chandeliers was for exactly this purpose: for drawing the fixture down with a hook on the end of a pole in order to maintain balance and control over the chandelier. Today, a large and heavy chandelier is increasingly likely to be fitted with an electric winch installed in the ceiling above it, and below the floorboards of the room above. The many fine chandeliers in the White House, for example, are presently being fitted, one by one, with these devices. Most cathedral chandeliers also have winches, installed so high up that they can hardly be seen. The required length of steel cable for lowering the fixture is stored in nearby roof space or between

the floorboards. Usually a safety line is also fitted, stretching from the bottom of the chandelier, up through the middle and out and upto the ceiling. Apart from acting as an extra support mechanism, should the main cable fail for any reason, it can also help to ensure that legal health and safety requirements are fulfilled when the chandelier is hung in a public space.

When you put up or take down a step ladder or platform in order to reach the chandelier, do this well away from the fitting and then move it into place. This will reduce the risk of accidentally knocking and damaging the chandelier. Support glass parts as you handle them, cupping them in your hand, for example, rather than gripping a narrow part that might snap under pressure. In an ideal situation, have someone below to whom you can pass the pieces, rather than having to climb down each time, and be sure that your helper is briefed about handling glass with care. Look for damage on each piece, and take care not to immerse mended glass (or indeed metal parts) in water – the glue may be water-soluble. Set aside any poorly or obtrusively mended parts to be delivered to a glass restorer.

As you unhook or remove each part, tie a label to it bearing a note of its location, and/or make a drawing and take notes to help you put the parts back in the same place after cleaning. You might also find it useful to take a photograph of the assembled chandelier, before you start dismantling it. This can be used as reference later. Parts that cannot be dismantled should be carefully wiped with a clean, barely damp cloth, or with a half-and-half mixture of industrial methylated spirits and distilled water, then dried carefully with a soft, lint-free cloth until they shine.

Leaders in the field of chandelier cleaning recommend dipping glass parts into a solution of warm water and a top-quality household detergent of the type designed for hand-washing domestic china and glass, or wiping with clean tufts of cotton wool dipped in a half-and-half mixture of industrial methylated spirits and distilled water. Then dry the pieces thoroughly and carefully with a soft, lint-free cloth. Rinsing soaped items in clean water before drying is a good idea, but experts vary in their views on whether this is strictly necessary. Do not put parts of your chandelier in the dishwasher.

Gently but thoroughly clean and dry each piece completely before starting the next, so as to avoid the risk of parts chipping each other in the washing solution. Allow yourself plenty of space in which to work. When you put down glass parts after cleaning them and before reassembling the chandelier, don't let them touch, and don't place them on a shiny, smooth surface where they might slip. A clean dishtowel or paper towel laid on the surface should help prevent any accidents.

When you reassemble your chandelier, consider wearing fine cotton or latex gloves to avoid leaving fingerprints on your newly cleaned glass. Consider your antique chandelier to be a bit like a jigsaw puzzle in that it has many parts which need to be slotted together in the right way. Unlike a jigsaw, however, it is possible to put a chandelier back together after cleaning with the pieces arranged very differently from the way they were before. This has happened so often over the decades and centuries, indeed, that antique dealers and restorers routinely expect to have to rearrange the parts of chandeliers they have bought in markets and auctions. One easy way of spotting that a chandelier has been incorrectly assembled – whether by you or by a previous owner – is if parts such as arms, spires, drops, or necklaces of beads touch each other. This almost certainly indicates an error. But the overriding question to ask when examining your fitting is simply whether it

Above: *Every part of the chandelier needs to be removed for washing, then carefully dried and reassembled. This is not always as straightforward as it might seem so it is often a good idea to make drawings, take a photograph, or make notes of the complete chandelier.*

Left: *The éclat of a crystal chandelier is quickly dimmed by even a thin layer of dust. Careful dusting with a feather duster or wiping with a barely damp cloth may be sufficient to clean it (always test a small area first to check you aren't removing a special finish), but if it is really grimy it will need washing. In most cases this will be necessary only once every few years.*

looks right. If, when you step back from your chandelier, it seems to you that its proportions and form, the arrangement of its arms and decorations, the point at which the arms are placed between the bottom and the top, are pleasing to the eye, then the chandelier is probably correctly assembled. If not, you can of course reassemble it differently, after cleaning, to your satisfaction.

The National Trust, which cares for numerous historic properties in England and Wales, cleans its chandeliers every winter, when properties are shut, and then carefully ties each one into a specially sewn bag of butter muslin in order to keep the dust off it until the spring when the property re-opens. This was also the traditional practice in grand houses that were only occupied for certain months of each year. However, unless you live in a particularly smutty city or have hung your chandelier in the kitchen, where it will be inclined to collect dirt more readily, with luck you will only need to dismantle and wash it every few years. In between, the application of a good quality feather or long-fibred duster (the National Trust uses pony-hair) may be sufficient to dislodge the dust from crevices, and careful cleaning with a vacuum cleaner fitted with a soft brush attachment may also be possible, but remember always use common sense when handling or touching a chandelier.

If you want your chandelier always to be spotless, do not have the time that is needed for regular maintenance and cleaning, or you are simply nervous about touching it, consider taking out a contract with a specialist cleaning company, who will pay you regular visits. You may also be able to arrange for them to test and change bulbs for you at regular intervals and before special events such as parties, when you want to be sure that a blown bulb will not spoil the effect of your beautiful chandelier. If you do employ a specialist firm to clean or repair a fitting, satisfy yourself that they have the required insurance in order to protect you, the chandelier, and themselves while the job is in hand.

Chandeliers made of materials other than glass can generally be cleaned by dusting, or by wiping carefully with a warm, barely damp cloth and then drying. Test a small area first to check that you will not thereby accidentally remove any special finish. In this case, or if in doubt, clean your chandelier with a dry duster or cloth.

TECHNICAL TIPS

One thing you need to be absolutely sure of, clearly, is that your chandelier is safe: that it will stay up, that it won't drop pieces on your head, and that it won't electrocute anyone or burn the house down. There are two basic factors in ensuring that, as far as possible, any chandelier or other light fitting is safe: common sense and professional expertise.

Large chandeliers naturally present greater potential problems than small ones. A large chandelier will be heavy and valuable, so the ceiling from which it is to be hung should be surveyed to establish if and how it will bear the load. Sometimes it is necessary to install a steel plate in the ceiling in order to spread the load across several structural members. You may also want to have an electric winch installed for raising and lowering the chandelier.

For the correct advice and a safe installation, you are almost certain to need the expertise of professionals: you can either co-ordinate a surveyor, structural engineer, builder, and electrician yourself, or you can employ the services of a specialist chandelier company to manage the entire project. If you have bought the chandelier through an auction house or from a knowledgeable dealer, they should be able to suggest or recommend a reputable company. Word of mouth is also a good advertisement for skilled professionals, though you should satisfy yourself of their competence, qualifications, insurance, and record by following this up with formal enquiries.

If you buy a large chandelier, antique or otherwise, from a specialist company that has cleaned and restored it, it may well not be wired for electricity. This is because different countries have different requirements in this respect. You have the choice of leaving it as it is and using it with candles, or of asking for it to be wired. In most countries, any company that owns a chandelier wired for electricity is responsible for the standard of the wiring when it is sold. Thus at least one leading chandelier company, Wilkinson, always rewires chandeliers that come into its possession, even in cases where they rewired the same fitting themselves only a few years earlier.

Glass chandeliers with solid arms, by their very nature, cannot be drilled for internal wiring; brass chandeliers sometimes can. Instead, discreet electrical wiring with a clear plastic coating can be run along the tops

of the arms and then secured by fine wire or contact adhesive; this can be removed later if not required and is invisible from below. The wiring is then run up the central core of the chandelier to the ceiling. In order to provide access for the wires to the core, it may be necessary to have a new arm plate or block (the solid part into which all the arms are slotted when a glass chandelier is assembled) specially made. The new plate will have an extra tiny hole on the stem side of each of the arm slots, through which the wire will then be threaded.

If you buy a chandelier from a market or junk shop, you should use common sense about rewiring, looking carefully to see if there are signs of wear or corrosion. By all means have it tested by an electrician or chandelier specialist, and if in doubt have it rewired. If the job is simple and you are experienced, you may be able to rewire it yourself. In electrical terms, of course, any chandelier is only as safe as the circuit of which it is part.

Various styles of electric "candle" are available from a number of sources. One possibility is a nylon candle into the top of which you screw a small bulb shaped to approximate a candle flame. Nylon candles are generally available in white, a creamy off-white, and a pale toffee colour imitating beeswax, and their shapes and lengths may vary. An alternative is the candle tube or sleeve: these generally take a less expensive bulb of a type more widely available, and come plain or with a dripping-wax effect.

An English company, McCloud Lighting, has patented another alternative – a form of electric light that actually flickers in response to moving air in the same way as a real candle flame. The effect is astonishingly realistic; it is also expensive to produce, as it requires an electronic starter and low frequency sensors. For safety in historic buildings, or where cost is not an issue, this kinetic light source offers the possibility of electric light with all the elusive, subtle charm (and none of the practical demands) of candlelight. It can be used just as effectively in a single candlestick as in a vast glittering crystal chandelier. Already installed in historic buildings such as Edinburgh Castle and Shakespeare's birthplace in Stratford-upon-Avon, it promises to be the favoured form of electric-powered lighting for chandeliers in the future.

Halogen lights are used in contemporary chandeliers where the transformer that controls the low voltage is accommodated in the design and located near the bulb. If the transformer is more than about 1m (3ft) from the bulb a number of problems can result, including overheating of the wires. In traditional crystal and other chandeliers, halogen bulbs are sometimes used to give additional uplighting (where the ceiling is exceptionally pretty, for example) or downlighting. They are only rarely used in place of candles with tungsten bulbs, because of the difficulty of accommodating the transformer and because the light is such a bright white.

If you want real candles for your chandelier, choose a good-quality brand and position the chandelier away from draughts. Air movement that causes one side of a candle to melt faster than the other (and thus to break the side of the wax bowl on the tip of the candle) is likely to cause dripping. It is also inadvisable to hang a chandelier near a wall, as static electricity generally has the effect of drawing smoke toward the wall, eventually causing sooty deposits. Besides draughts, another possible cause of dripping and smoking candles is poor quality (incompletely refined) paraffin wax of the type used in the manufacture of some cheap candles. Good-quality candles often have a quantity of stearin mixed with the wax, which gives a cleaner flame but marginally less light. Stearin used to be extracted from whale blubber, but is now usually obtained from palm trees in Asia. Best-quality candles are through-moulded – made by pouring wax into a mould – rather than manufactured from compacted powdered wax, but this process is slower and therefore more expensive. But because the finished candle has no air trapped between powder particles, it will burn more evenly. Another cause of dripping is the use by some manufacturers of inappropriate wicks, which either fail to draw up the wax effectively or burn too quickly. Wicks are made from a variety of fibres with different weaves and capillary actions. A candle is a balanced system of burn-melt-suck-burn and so on: if wax, wick, or the external environment disturbs this balance then the candle will operate inefficiently. Until World War II, at least one leading manufacturer (Price's) used to make candles to suit all the varying climates in the world – but sadly no longer. Today, once you find a type that performs well in your home you would be well advised to stick with it.

Left and right: *Spare drops of all shapes and sizes can be found in antique shops or markets, or you can have replacements made specially to complete your chandelier.*

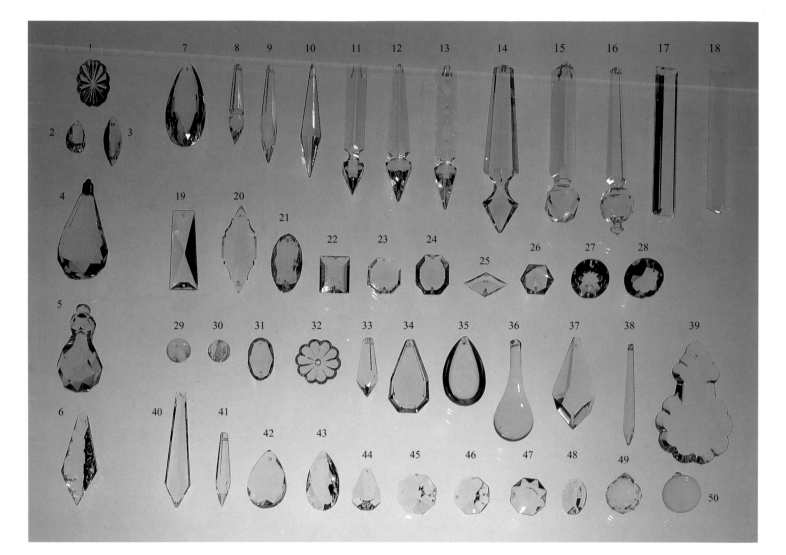

18th-century English-style drops

1   Sunray button
2   Link pear
3   Georgian oval or diamond
4   Early metal capped pear drop
5   Facetted knob drop
6   Kite drop

19th-century English-style drops

7   Pear drop
8   Waisted icicle
9   Round icicle
10   Triangular icicle
11   Plain albert
12   Tapered albert
13   Cut back albert
14   Spear drop
15   Drumstick
16   Osler faceted ball and shaft drop

17   Rule drop
18   Prism
19   Coffin
20   Shaped coffin
21   Oval button
22   Rule button
23   Octagonal flatback 8 cut
24   Octagonal flatback 16 cut
25   Diamond
26   Hexagonal flatback
27   Round double point button
28   Round flatback button

Continental-style drops

29   Plain bead
30   Faceted bead
31   Swedish oval
32   Rosette
33   Bomb drop

34   French pear
35   Plain or uncut pear
36   Tear drop
37   Bohemian pear
38   Swedish icicle
39   French slab drop

Modern drops

40   Waterford drop
41   Icicle
42   Moulded pear
43   Swarovski pear
44   Square cut pear
45   Garnet cut octagon (Swarovski)
46   Standard cut octagon
47   Moulded octagonal flatback
48   Modern oval
49   Faceted ball
50   Plain ball

There are hundreds of different styles of drops and buttons – illustrated above are 50 of the most popular, courtesy of Wilkinson, London.

GLOSSARY

A

ADAM STYLE
A neoclassical style, light, airy, elegant and usually English, named after the Scottish architect and designer Robert Adam (1728–92).

ARM
The light-bearing part of a chandelier, also sometimes known as a branch.

ARM PLATE
A metal plate (usually brass), or occasionally (as on some old Venetian chandeliers) a wooden block, placed on the stem, into which the arms slot.

B

BAG
A bag of crystal drops formed by strings hanging from a circular frame and looped back into the centre underneath, associated especially with early American crystal and Regency-style crystal chandeliers.

BALUSTER
A turned wood or moulded brass stem forming the axis of a chandelier, with alternating narrow and bulbous parts of varying widths.

BEAD
A glass drop with a hole drilled right through it.

BLANK
A solid piece of glass that is ready to be cut or otherwise fashioned by some other method into an element that will eventually make up a chandelier.

BOBECHE
A dish fitted just below the candle nozzle, designed to catch drips of wax. Also known as a drip pan.

BRANCH
Another term for a light-bearing arm, holding a candle or bulb.

C

CANDELABRA
Not to be confused with chandeliers, candelabra are candlesticks, usually branched, designed to stand on tables or, if large, the floor.

CANDLEBEAM
A cross made from two wooden beams, with one or more cups and prickets at each end for securing candles. The earliest known form of domestic chandelier, it was found only in wealthy homes.

CANDLE NOZZLE
The small cup into which the end of the candle is slotted.

CANOPY
An inverted shallow dish at the top of a chandelier (and sometimes at intermediate points), from which festoons of beads are often suspended, lending a flourish to the top of the fitting.

CAGE
An arrangement found in many French, French-style and Baltic chandeliers in which the central stem supporting arms and decorations is replaced by a metal structure, usually open, leaving the centre clear for candles and further embellishments.

CORONA
Another term for a crown-style chandelier.

CROWN
A circular chandelier reminiscent of a crown, usually of gilded metal or brass, and often with upstanding decorative elements.

CRYSTAL
Glass with a lead content that gives it special qualities of clarity, resonance and softness (making it especially suitable for cutting), also known as lead crystal.

D

DRIP PAN
The dish fitted just below the candle nozzle, designed to catch drips of wax. Known in America as a bobeche.

DROP

A small piece of glass usually cut into one of many shapes (some illustrated opposite) and drilled at one end so that it can be hung from the chandelier with a brass pin. A chain drop is drilled at both ends so that a series can be hung together to form a necklace or festoon.

DUTCH

Also known as Flemish, a style of brass chandelier with a bulbous baluster and arms curving down around a low-hung ball. Made fashionable across Europe and the New World by Dutch chandeliers of the fifteenth, sixteenth, seventeenth and eighteenth centuries, possibly the most enduring popular chandelier.

E

EARLY

In Europe, early is used to denote chandeliers made before the emergence of the Dutch or Flemish form in the seventeenth century, generally of wood, brass and other metals. Many were destroyed during the Reformation. In America, early types of naive chandelier, made of tin sheet or with wire arms attached to a wooden baluster, continued to be made well into the nineteenth century, and again today.

ELECTROLIER

A chandelier, usually nineteenth century, designed to be powered by electricity.

F

FESTOON

An arrangement of glass drops or beads draped and hung across or down a glass chandelier, or sometimes a piece of solid glass shaped into a swag. Also known as a garland.

FINIAL

Usually the final flourish at the very bottom of the stem of any chandelier, though Venetian glass chandeliers often have little finials hanging from glass rings on the arms.

G

GASOLIER

A chandelier powered by gas.

H

HALOGEN

Clean, bright white light supplied by tiny low-voltage bulbs, each requiring a transformer to adapt the electricity supply.

HOOP

A circular metal support for arms, usually on a Regency-style or other chandelier decorated with glass pieces. Also known as a ring.

I

ICICLE

A long glass drop, tapering and pointed at the end.

L

LAMP

As used by the lighting industry, synonymous with bulb.

LEAD CRYSTAL

See Crystal.

LUSTRE

Another word for chandelier.

M

MODERN

Any chandelier made since the early twentieth century, but more usually a chandelier whose appearance and style is forward-looking rather than historical. A new chandelier in a historical style is termed reproduction.

MOULDED

The process by which a glass piece and/or its decoration is shaped by being blown into a mould (rather than cut).

N

NEOCLASSICAL STYLE

Eighteenth-century style of (usually) glass chandelier featuring many delicate arms, spires and strings of beads, the ultimate in airy elegance.

NOZZLE

The small cup-like attachment at the end of a chandelier arm into which the candle fits snugly so that it stands upright.

O

OPALINE

Milky, that is translucent rather than transparent.

P

PRICKET

A metal spike to secure a candle, found mostly on early, primitive and neo-rustic chandeliers, powered by candles rather than electricity.

PRISM

A straight, many-sided drop.

R

REGENCY STYLE

A frequently massive style of chandelier with a multitude of drops. Above a hoop rise strings of beads that diminish in size and attach at the top to form a canopy. A bag, concentric rings of pointed glass icicle drops, forms a waterfall beneath. The stem is usually completely hidden.

REPRODUCTION

A newly made chandelier in a historical style.

ROCK CRYSTAL

A form of quartz used for the earliest, fabulously costly, forms of crystal chandelier.

ROSSO AMERICANO

A shade of red Venetian glass, so called because of its popularity with American tourists and buyers in the later nineteenth century.

S

SCONCE

A wall-mounted lighting fixture, often complementary to a chandelier in form, style and materials.

SHADE

A tall, tulip-shaped glass cup, open at the base and sometimes decorated with engraved or painted patterns, placed over a candle on a chandelier to protect it from draughts.

SODA GLASS

A type of glass used typically in Venetian chandeliers (as opposed to English, American and other cut-glass chandeliers, which are made from a type of glass that contains lead). Soda glass remains plastic for longer when heated, and can therefore be shaped into elegantly curving leaves and flowers.

SPIRE

A tall spike of glass, round in section or flat sided, sometimes notched and often supported by a glass arm, which contributes to the glittering effect of Adam and neoclassical crystal chandeliers.

STEM

The central support of a chandelier, to which arms and decorative elements may be attached, made from wood, metal or a metal rod clad in sections of glass. On antique glass chandeliers, the latter often prove to have been replaced in the wrong order after earlier cleaning.

T

TENT

A tent-shaped structure on the upper part of a late eighteenth- or early nineteenth-century glass chandelier, formed from necklaces of drops attached at the top to a canopy and at the bottom to a larger ring or hoop of metal. The drops diminish in size as they rise, creating an illusion of greater height. The tent is most usually associated with Regency-style chandeliers, in which the structure is completed by a bag or waterfall suspended below the ring.

V

VENETIAN

Strictly speaking, a glass chandelier made on the island of Murano, Venice, but generally used to describe any chandelier in Venetian style or *façon de Venice*, of which many were and are made in other countries throughout the world.

W

WATERFALL

Concentric rings of icicle drops suspended beneath the hoop and tent of a Regency chandelier.

DIRECTORY

SHOPS, MANUFACTURERS, AND DESIGNERS

Europe:

Anthony Redmile Ltd
The Furniture Cave
533 King's Road
London SW10 0TZ
UK
Tel: +44 (0)20 7351 3813
Fax: +44 (0)20 7352 8131
email: sales@redmile.co.uk
www.redmile.co.uk

Baccarat
37 Old Bond Street
London W1X 3AE
UK
Tel: +44 (0)20 7409 7767
Fax: +44 (0)20 7409 7177

Baccarat
30 bis rue de Paradis
BP 89
75010 Paris Cedex 10
France
Tel: +33 1 47 70 64 30
Fax: +33 1 42 46 97 08

Barovier & Toso
Fondamenta Vetrai 28
30141 Murano
Venezia
Italy
Tel: +39 041 739049
Fax: +39 041 5274385
email: barovier@barovier.com
www.barovier.com.

Bella Figura
G5 Chelsea Harbour
Design Centre
Lots Road
London SW10 0XE
UK
Tel: +44 (0)20 7376 4564
Fax: +44 (0)20 7376 4565

Carlton Davidson
507 King's Road
London SW10 0TX
UK
Tel: +44 (0)20 7795 0905
Fax: +44 (0)20 7795 0904
email: natalie@carltondavidson.co.uk

Catalytico
25 Montpelier Street
London SW7 1HF
UK
Tel: +44 (0)20 7225 1720
Fax: +44 (0)20 7225 3740
email: catalyn@dircon.co.uk

Christopher Wray Lighting
591–593 King's Road
London SW6 2YW
Branches around the UK
Trade enquiries: +44 (0)20 7751 8702
General enquiries: +44 (0)20 7751 8701
email: sales@christopher-wray.com
www.christopher-wray.com

Delomosne & Son Ltd
Contact details in Restoration, Cleaning and
Installation Specialists

Eurolounge
11 Northburgh Street
London EC1V 0AH
UK
Tel: +44 (0)20 7792 5477
Fax: +44 (0)20 7250 0311

Flos Ltd UK
31 Lisson Grove
London NW1 6UB
UK
Tel: 020 7258 0600
Fax: 020 7723 7005

Fritz Fryer Antique Lighting
12 Brookend Street
Ross-on-Wye
Herefordshire HR9 7EG
UK
Tel: +44 (0)1989 567416
Fax: +44 (0)1989 566742
email: fryer@wyenet.co.uk
www.fritzfryer.co.uk

Jim Lawrence Traditional Ironwork Ltd
Scotland Hall Farm
Stoke by Nayland
Colchester
Essex CO6 4QG
UK
Tel: +44 (0)1206 263459
Fax: +44 (0)1206 262166
email: sales@jim-lawrence.co.uk
www.jim-lawrence.co.uk

Kensington Lighting Company
59 Kensington Church Street
London W8 4BA
UK
Tel: +44 (0)20 7938 2405
Fax: +44 (0)20 7937 5915

Laura Ashley
27 Bagleys Lane
Fulham
London SW6 2QA
UK
Tel: +44 (0)20 7880 5100
Fax: +44 (0)20 7880 5200
www.lauraashley.com

McCloud Lighting
19/20 Chelsea Harbour Design Centre
Lots Road
London SW10 0XE
UK
Tel: +44 (0)20 7352 1533
Fax:+44 (0)20 7352 1570
email: contactus@mccloud.co.uk
www.mccloud.co.uk

M. E. Crick Chandeliers
Associated with Denton Antiques
166–168 Kensington Church Street
London W8 4BN
UK
Tel: +44 (0)20 7229 5866
Fax: +44 (0)20 7792 1073
email: dentonantiques@ukgateway.net

Madeline Boulesteix
2 Carlton Mansions
387 Coldharbour Lane
London SW9 8QD
UK
Tel: +44 (0)20 7737 8171

Mallett & Son (Antiques) Ltd
141 New Bond Street
London W1S 2BS
UK
Tel: +44 (0)20 7499 7411
email: antiques@mallett.co.uk
www.mallettantiques.com

Preciosa-Lustry
Head Office
Opletalova 17
Jablonec nad Nisou 466 67
The Czech Republic
Tel: +420 428 415 111
Fax: +420 428 311 761
email: sales@preciosa.com

Price's Patent Candles Co Ltd
16 Hudson Road
Elms Farm Industrial Estate
Bedford MK41 0LZ
UK
Tel: +44 (0)1234 320004
Fax: +44 (0)1234 325664
email: info@prices.candles.co.uk
www.prices-candles.co.uk

Pruskin Gallery
73 Kensington Church Street
London W8 4BG
UK
Tel: +44 (0)20 7937 1994

Richard Taylor Designs
Unit 17, Thames House
Southbank Commercial Centre
140 Battersea Park Road
London SW11 4NB
UK
Tel: +44 (0)20 7720 2772
Fax:+44 (0)20 7720 3772
email: enquiries@richardtaylordesigns.co.uk
www.1-1.net/richardtaylordesigns

Stuart Interiors Ltd
Barrington Court
Barrington
Ilminster
Somerset TA19 0NQ
UK
Tel: +44 (0)1460 240349
Fax: +44 (0)1460 242069
email: stuart_interiors@hotmail.com
www.stuartinteriors.ltd.uk

Trade Routes
57 Cambridge Street
London SW1V 4PS
UK
Tel: +44 (0)20 7821 8588
Fax: +44 (0)20 7821 8589

Vetreria De Majo Srl
Fondamenta Navagero Andrea
Murano 29
30141 Venezia
Italy
Tel: +39 041 739988
Fax: +39 041 739703
Show room: +39 041 5274667
email:demajomurano.com
www.demajomurano.com

Wilkinson plc
1 Grafton Street
London W1X 3LB
UK
Tel: +44 (0)20 7495 2477
Fax: +44 (0)20 7491 1737

Woka Lamps Vienna
Palais Breuner
Singerstrasse 16
A-1010 Vienna
Austria
Tel: +43 1 5132912
Fax: +43 1 5138505
email: woka@wokalamps.com
www.wokalamps.com

Wonderful Lamps
2/24 Chelsea Harbour
Design Centre
Chelsea Harbour
London SW10 0XE
UK
Tel:+44 (0)20 7351 4669
Fax: +44 (0)20 7352 3898

North America:

A & W Lighting
1124 Hillcrest Road
Mobile, AL 36695
USA
Tel: +1 334 607 0099
Fax: +1 334 607 0093

Baccarat
625 Madison Avenue - 59th Street
New York, NY 10022
USA
Tel: +1 212 826 4100
Fax: +1 212 826 5043

Blaine's Lighting
12312 Saratoga Sunnyvale Road
Saratoga, CA 95070-0308
USA
Tel: +1 408 252 7400
Fax: +1 408 252 1815
www.blaineslighting.com

Capitol Lighting
2851 US Highway 1
Trenton
NJ 08648
USA
Tel: +1 609 882 2119

Crest Lighting Studio
13400 Cicero Ave
Midlothian
IL 60445
USA
Tel: +1 708 597 4220

Crystal Farm
18 Antelope Road
Redstone,
CO 81623
USA
Tel: +1 970 963 2350
Fax: +1 970 963 0709

Empire Lighting
8400 Woodbine Ave
Markham, Ontario
Canada L3R 4N7
Tel: +1 905 513 1073
Fax: +1 905 513 6323

Fischer Gambino
637 Royal Street
New Orleans
USA
Tel: +1 504 524 9067
Fax: +1 504 581 7946
www.fischergambino.com

Furlong Lamp & Shade Outlet
760 York Road
Furlong, PA 18925
USA
Tel: +1 215 794 7444

Galaxie Lighting
3663 S. Main St
Salt Lake City, UT 84115
USA
Tel: +1 801 262 5531
Fax: +1 801 262 5654
email: galaxielighting@xmission.com

Gem Electric
11400 S. Cicero
Alsip, IL 60803
USA
Tel: +1 708 597 9600
Fax: +1 708 597 9640

George Kovacs Lighting Inc
67-25 Otto Road
Glendale, NY 11385
USA
Tel: +1 718 628 5201
Fax: +1 718 628 5212
email: info@georgekovacslighting.com
www.georgekovacslighting.com

H A Framburg & Co
941 Cernan Drive
Bellwood, IL 60104
USA
Tel: +1 800 796 5514
email: Framburg@Framburg.com
www.framburg.com

House of Lights
49560 Van Dyke
Utica, MI 48317
USA
Tel: +1 810 739 9440
Fax: +1 810 739 9588
email: Sales@HouseOfLightsUSA.com
www.houseoflightsusa.com

James R Moder Crystal Chandelier Inc
P.O. Box 420346
Dallas, TX 75342-0346
USA
Tel: +1 800 663 1232
Fax: +1 214 742 4088
email: crystal@jamesmoder.com
www.jamesmodes.com

Lamp & Shade Works
160 Delsea Drive
Sewell, NJ 08080
USA
Tel: +1 856 401 2630
Fax: +1 856 401 2631
email: jovin160@aol.com

Lamps Plus
20250 Plummer St
Chatsworth, CA 91311
USA
Tel: +1 818 886 5267
Fax: +1 818 772 1569
email: Sales@LampsPlus.com
www.lampsplus.com

Lighting Inc
6628 Gulf Freeway
Houston
TX 77087
USA
Tel: +1 713 641 6628

Lighting Superstore
678 Route 17 N
Paramus, NJ 07652
USA
Tel: +1 201 445 4700
Fax: +1 201 445 2338

Lighting Unlimited
11760 Parklawn Drive
Rockville, MD 20852
USA
Tel: +1 301 468 3500
Fax: +1 301 468 3886

Michigan Chandelier
190 Last Maple
Troy, MI 48083
USA
Tel: +1 248 583 3200
Fax: +1 248 583 9353

Nesle Inc
151 East 57th Street
New York, NY 10022
USA
Tel: +1 212 755 0515
Fax: +1 212 644 2583
email: nesle@earthlink.net
www.dir-dd.com/nesle.html

Nowell's Inc
P.O.Box 295
490 Gate 5 Road
Sausalito, CA 94965
USA
Tel: +1 415 332 4933
email: sauslamp@aol.com
www.nowells-inc.com

Period Lighting Fixtures Inc
River Road
North Adams, MA 01247
USA
Tel: +1 413 664 7141
www.periodlighting.com

Richardson Lighting
7070 San Pedro
San Antonio, TX 78216
USA
Tel: +1 210 822 5100
Fax: +1 210 822 5124

Schonbek Worldwide Lighting
61 Industrial Blvd.
Plattsburgh, NY 12901-1908
USA
Tel: +1 518 563 7500
Fax: +1 518 563 4228
email: webmaster@schonbek.com
www.schonbek.com

Unilight Ltd
5530 St-Patrick Street
Montreal
Quebec
Canada H4E 1A8
Tel: +1 514 769 1533
Fax: +1 514 769 8858
email: info@unilight.ca
www.unilight.ca

RESTORATION, CLEANING, AND INSTALLATION SPECIALISTS

All of these companies operate a worldwide service

**Chandelier Cleaning
and Restoration Services Ltd**
Gypsy Mead
Fyfield
Essex CM5 0RB
UK
Tel: +44 (0)1277 899444
Fax: +44 (0)1277 899642
email: enquiries@cgp.demon.co.uk
www.chandeliergroup.com

Delomosne & Son Ltd
Court House
North Wraxall
Chippenham
Wiltshire SN14 7AD
UK
Tel: +44 (0)1225 891505
Fax: +44 (0)1225 891907
email: Timosborne@delomosne.co.uk
www.delomosne.co.uk

Wilkinson plc
5 Catford Hill
London SE6 4NU
UK
Tel: +44 (0)20 8314 1080
Fax: +44 (0)20 8690 1524

SPECIAL COMMISSIONS

Bloxam De Matteis
1.03 Oxo Tower Wharf
Barge House Street
London SE1 9PH
UK
Tel: +44 (0)20 7633 9494
email: bloxam-dematteis@lineone.net
Lindsay Bloxam Design also undertakes individual pieces and can be contacted at the above address or the following e-mail address.
email: info@lindsaybloxam-design.co.uk

Chiho Hitomi
78 Castelnau
Barnes
London SW13 9EX
UK
Tel: +44 (0)20 8395 5515

Chihuly Inc
Chihuly Studio
(closed to the public)
1111 NW 50th Street
Seattle
WA 98107-5120
USA
Tel: +1 206 781 8707
Fax: +1 206 781 1906
www.chihuly.com

Jo Whiting
UK
Mobile Tel: 0973 829698
Fax: +44 (0)20 8715 2759

Jim Lawrence Traditional Ironwork Ltd
Contact details in Shops and Manufacturers

Kevin McCloud
McCloud Lighting
Contact details in Shops and Manufacturers

Tom Kirk
13c Camberwell Church St
London SE5 8TR
UK
Tel/fax: +44 (0)20 7780 9288
email: tomkirk@excite.co.uk

Sharon Marston
Studio 38
21 Clerkenwell Green
London EC1R 0DP
Tel/fax: +44 (0)20 7490 7495
email: enquiries@sharonmarston.com
www.sharonmarston.com

Ingo Maurer GmbH
Kaiserstrasse 47
80801 Munchen
Germany
Email: postmaster@ingo-maurer.com
www.ingo-maurer.com

FLEA MARKETS

Europe:

La Batte
Liège
Belgium
Open: Sunday 8am - 2pm
Thought of as the oldest street market in Europe,
full of stalls offering a variety of items.

Mother Redcap's Market
Back Lane
Dublin 8
Ireland
Open: Friday to Sunday 10am - 5:30pm
A large, indoor market in the heart of Dublin, stalls
selling locally produced goods and antiques.

Covent Garden Market
41 The Market The Piazza
London WC2E 8RF
England
www.coventgardenmarket.co.uk
Open: Monday: Antiques and collectibles
           Tuesday to Sunday: Arts and crafts
Located in the old apple market, a colourful market
with a variety of stalls.

Place du Jeu-de-Balle
Brussels
Belgium
Open: Daily: 7am - 2pm
An interesting selection of second-hand items,
located in the Marolles district.

Waterlooplein
Amsterdam
The Netherlands
Open: Monday to Saturday
300 stalls located behind Amsterdam's Town Hall,
particularly good in the summer for antiques.

Feira da Ladra
Lisbon
Portugal
Open: Tuesday morning
           Saturday: 7am - 6pm
Open-air market in the Alfambra district, selling
bric a brac, Portuguese crafts and food.

Porta Portese
Rome
Italy
Open: Sunday 5am - 2pm
The largest general market in Rome, selling both
used and new items.

March aux Puces
Paris
France
Open: Saturday to Monday: 7:30 - 7pm
An old market located in St-Ouen, around 3,000
stalls selling bric a brac, pieces of furniture and
antiques.

Strabe des 17 Juli
Berlin
Germany
Open: Saturday & Sunday 11.00 - 17.00
A popular market, with a wide range of stalls.

North America:

Brimfield Outdoor Antiques Show
Brimfield
Massachusetts
Open: Three times a year for a week, during May,
July and September.
A popular flea market, selling goods that range
from paperbacks to antiques.

Daytona Flea Market
Tomoka Farms Rd
Daytona
FL 32124
Open: Friday to Sunday 8am - 5pm
One of the largest markets in Florida with 1,000
covered outdoor booths and some antique dealers.
Indoors.

Austin County Flea Market
9500 Hwy 290 East
Austin
Texas
Open: Saturday and Sunday 9am - 5pm
Lots to browse through from fresh produce to
antiques.

San Jose Market
12000 Berryessa Rd
San Jose
CA 95118
USA
Open: Wednesday to Sunday dawn to dusk
This huge market has over 2,000 booths.

Saint Clair Flea Market
404 Old Weston Road
Toronto
ON M6N 3B1
Canada
Open: Saturday and Sunday 10 am - 6pm
Every kind of merchandise can be found in this
market varying from furniture to fashion items.

www.fleamarketguide.com is a useful resource to
find other flea markets in USA and Canada.

INDEX

ACKNOWLEDGMENTS

One of the great pleasures of researching this book has been making contact with so many people who are as fascinated as I am by chandeliers, and who have been so enthusiastic and generous with their time, information and images. To all the following I offer a huge thank you – Elizabeth Hilliard.

Maggie Alderson; Mr and Mrs Richard Anderson; Laura Ashley; Gail Bardhan, Rakow Research Library, The Corning Museum of Glass, New York (tel: +1 607 974 8166); Barovier & Toso; Juliet Beaumont; Eileen Schonbek Beer, Schonbek; Corrado Bertin; Lindsay Bloxam and Bloxam De Matteis; Madeleine Boulesteix; The Dean and Chapter of Bristol Cathedral; Paul Brown; Felicity Bryan and Michéle Topham; Lynn Bryan; Stephen Calloway; Catalytico; Ken Clark, Chihuly Studio archives; Colonial Williamsburg; Dr Maureen Dillon; Henrietta Edwards, Assistant to the Deputy Surveyor of the Queen's Works of Art; Judith Elsdon and Anne Armitage, the American Museum in Britain, Bath (tel: +44 (0)1225 460503); Rinskokatolicka Farnost; Donald L. Fennimore, Winterthur Museum, Delaware (tel: +1 302 888 4600); Bella Figura; Belinda Fisher, Anne Stabler Associates; Flos; Fritz Fryer; Alice Cooney Frelinghuysen and Jessie McNab, the Metropolitan Museum, New York (+1 212 879 5500); Piers Gough; Bridget Graham, Christopher Wray Lighting; Auberon Hedgecoe; Giulia Hetherington; The Great Eastern Dining Room; The Great Eastern Hotel; Heather and David Hilliard; Michael Holy, Unilight; Michael Hunter, Osborne House; Peter Hutchison, Historic Metallurgy Society; Dr Edward Impey, Hampton Court Palace (tel: +44 (0)20 8781 9500); George Kovacs; Dwight Lanmon; Jim Lawrence; James Lomax and Antony Wells-Cole, Temple Newsam, Leeds City Art Galleries (tel: +44 (0)113 264 7321); Elaine Louie; Kevin McCloud and Sarah Howarth, McCloud Lighting and Victor Chinnery; Lara Maiklem; Veteria De Majo; Mallet; Sharon Marston (tel/fax: 020 7490 7495; www.sharonmarston.com); Ingo Maurer; Barbara Mellor; Martin Mortimer; Stewart Nardi, The Chandelier Group; Pascaline Noack , Baccarat; National Art Library, London; The National Trust at Queen Anne's Gate, London (+44 (0)20 7222 9251; www.nationaltrust.org.uk), and the many National Trust properties we consulted; Gaia Di Palma; Luciona Peidicini, Museo di Capodimonte; James Peto, the Design Museum, London (tel: +44 (0)20 7403 6933); Elizabeth Pink, The Whitworth Art Gallery, Manchester (tel: +44 (0)161 275 7450); Preciosa-Lustry; Michael Pruskin, The Pruskin Gallery, London (tel: +44 (0)20 7937 1994); Sarah Riddick; Ronald Swan, The Royal Foundation of St Katharine (tel: +44 (0)20 7790 3540 by appointment only); William Selka; Probar Shah, Science Museum; Jane Shadel Spillman, The Corning Museum of Glass, New York; Helen Stallion; David Storrar, Historic Scotland; Stuart Interiors; Fratelli Toso, Murano; Tower of London (+44 (0)20 7680 9004); Victoria & Albert Museum, London (tel: +44 (0)20 794 2531); Susan Watson; Neil Watton and Chris Bennet, Wonderful Lamps; Claire Waite Brown; The White House Heritage Trust; Christopher Wilk; David Wilkinson, Wilkinson plc; Emily Wilkinson.

PICTURE CREDITS
Key: b: bottom; t: top; l: left; r: right

Abode: 26, 35 tl, 35 tr, 43, 87; Laura Ashley: 61; Axiom Photographic Agency: 187; Baccarat: 114; Barovier and Toso: 69, 72–73, 80; Bloxam & De Matteis: 139; Lindsay Bloxam: 154 tl, 156, 168; Camera Press: 60 t; Chihuly Studio: 174,176 tl, 177, 178 tl, 178–179, 179; Crown Copyright: Historic Royal Palaces: 41, 126; Danske Kongers Kronologiske Samling: 13; FLOS: 144, 156–157, 165; Great Eastern Hotel: 162; Historic Scotland, Edinburgh: 29; Hotel Cipriani: 75 tr; Houses & Interiors: Jake Fitzjones 108 tr; Michael Harris 103; Ingo Maurer: 160, 161, 180 t, 180 b, 181; The Interior Archive: Fernando Bengoechea 140–141; Tim Beddow 74, 117, 182; Tim Clinch 71 t, 82–83, 112; Ken Hayden 104, 109; Inside: C Sarraman 17, 169; Simon McBride 28, 93, 101, 107, 108 tl, 113 tl; Eduardo Munoz 106; Christopher Simon Sykes 38, 141; Simon Upton 2, 92 tl,96, 189; Wayne Vincent 110; Fritz von der Schulenburg 7, 36, 44, 52–53, 54, 55; 57; 59 tr, 64, 70, 85, 86, 100, 102, 102–103, 114–115, 119, 123, 124, 137, 147, 167, 188; Luke White 11; Henry Wilson 40, 75 tl, 81, 172; Andrew Wood 16, 33, 158, 183, 186; Peter Woloszynski 36–37, 146; International Interiors: Paul Ryan 19, 60 b, 97, 113 tr, 152; IPC: Country Homes and Interiors/Mel Yates 151; Homes & Gardens/Caroline Arber 89; Christopher Drake 98; Winfried Heinze 14; Verity Welstead 166; Living Etc/JP Masclet 192; Ray Main/Mainstream: Back cover, 12, 90, 91, 92 tr, 94 tl, 94–95, 95 tr, 111, 125, 154 tr, 163, 172–173, 175, 184–185, 194–195, 197; Ray Main/Mainstream/designer Babylon Design front cover, 159, 184, 196; Ray Main/Mainstream/designer Yoram Eshkol-Rovach 5, 135; Ray Main/Mainstream/light designer Ingo Maurer 159 t; Ray Main/Mainstream/designer Tejo Remy 134, 150, 164; Sharon Marston: 176 tr; McCloud Lighting: 27, 63, 65, 145; Martin Mortimer: 127; Narratives: Jan Baldwin 25; Polly Wreford 20; National Trust Photographic Library: Peter Aprahamian 116; Nadia MacKenzie 50, 122; J Pipkin 47; Andreas von Einsiedel 18–19; 45, 46, 49, 62, 68; Octopus Publishing Group Ltd: Sebastian Hedgecoe 6, 22, 23, 30, 30–31, 32, 48, 58, 66–67, 120–121, 133, 138–139, 170–171; Nicholas Kane 32; Luciano Pedicini:148; Pictor International 99; Preciosa Lustry: 21, 59 tl; Red Cover: Brian Harrison 56; Andrew Twort 15, 39, 142–143; Andreas von Einsiedel 88; Rinskokatolicka Farnost: 149; The Royal Pavilion, Brighton: 130, 131; Schonbek Chandeliers: 105; Stuart Interiors: 24; Unknown 52, 190, 193; Veteria de Majo: 71 b, 76, 77; Deidi von Schaewen: 8–9, 10, 78–79, 84, 118, 132, 136, 170; The White House Historical Association: 128, 128–129; Elizabeth Whiting Associates: 42, 51; Wilkinsons: 191, 198; Courtesy, Winterthur Museum: 34; Christopher Wray Lighting: 140, 153, 155.